FLOWING WITH THE PEARL RIVER

MEMOIR OF A RED CHINA GIRL

AMY CHAN ZHOU

SANTA
MONICA
PRESS
TEEN

Published by Santa Monica Press LLC
P.O. Box 850
Solana Beach, CA 92075
1-800-784-9553
www.santamonicapress.com
books@santamonicapress.com

Printed in the United States

ISBN-13 978-1-59580-136-4 (hardcover)
          978-1-59580-106-7 (paperback)
          978-1-59580-782-3 (ebook)

Publisher's Cataloging-in-Publication data

Names: Zhou, Amy Chan, author.
Title: Flowing with the Pearl River : memoir of a red China girl / by Amy Chan Zhou.
Description: Solana Beach, CA: Santa Monica Press, 2022.
Identifiers: ISBN: 978-1-59580-106-7 (print) | 978-1-59580-782-3 (ebook)
Subjects: LCSH Zhou, Amy Chan. | Chinese Americans--Biography. | Chinese--United States--Biography. | Immigrants--China--Biography. | Immigrants--United States--Biography. | Communism--China--History. | China--Politics and government. | BISAC YOUNG ADULT NONFICTION / Biography & Autobiography / Cultural, Ethnic & Regional | YOUNG ADULT NONFICTION / Family / Multigenerational | YOUNG ADULT NONFICTION / History / Asia | YOUNG ADULT NONFICTION / Social Topics / Emigration & Immigration | YOUNG ADULT NONFICTION / Social Science / Politics & Government | YOUNG ADULT NONFICTION / People & Places / United States / Asian American
Classification: LCC E184.C5 Z46 2022 | DDC 973.04951/092--dc23

Cover and interior design and production by Future Studio
Cover image: "The People's Communes Are Good" courtesy of The IISH collection, www.chineseposters.net

CONTENTS

Chapter 1. My Grandparents' Love 7
Chapter 2. My Mother and My Father 15
Chapter 3. The Fate of Being Labeled
            Landlord Class 25
Chapter 4. From the "Great Leap Forward"
            to the "Great Famine" 29
Chapter 5. My Father Meets My Mother 37
Chapter 6. Endless Political Campaigns:
            People Against People 41
Chapter 7. "Re-education" in Labor Camps 45
Chapter 8. Single Mother Surviving
            in Guangzhou City 53
Chapter 9. The Start of the Cultural Revolution 59
Chapter 10. A Vagrant Life 65
Chapter 11. Rejoining My Mother
            and Fighting for a Residence Permit 77
Chapter 12. The Red Shoes........................ 85
Chapter 13. A Wild Countryside Girl 95
Chapter 14. Working for a Point System 105
Chapter 15. A School without Classrooms 113
Chapter 16 My Furry Friends 129
Chapter 17. The Seven Escapes.................... 141
Chapter 18. Arrival in Hong Kong.................. 155
Chapter 19. The "Spy Girl" 161
Chapter 20 Paternal Grandmother's Last Wish 167
Chapter 21. The Campaign to Destroy
            the "Four Olds"........................ 173
Chapter 22. Public Accusation Meetings........... 181
Chapter 23. Capricious Fate 195

Chapter 24. A Little Capitalist Trader 201
Chapter 25. The End of Mao's Era 207
Chapter 26. Leaving China 213
Chapter 27. Family Reunion in Hong Kong 221
Chapter 28. Starting a New Life in the USA 237
Chapter 29. Visiting China 241
Chapter 30. Gratitude. 251

Author's Note 257
Acknowledgments 259

APPENDIX A. Chronology of
    Chinese Political Campaigns
    from 1949–1978 260
APPENDIX B. Family Tree 264
APPENDIX C. The Point System 265

Glossary 266
About the Author 272

WHEN I WAS YOUNG, each time my family's older generation told me something about the past, I took it for granted and most times did not pay attention. Years passed by, and I too, became a mother. Every time I visited my mother's home in Brooklyn, New York, she would sit in front of her old Singer sewing machine, using her rough fingers to measure a piece of cloth. Her wrinkled hands reminded me of how much she had gone through, and yet she insisted on making pants for my children.

While she was sewing, she spoke simply, yet disjointedly. Her miserable past experiences included the Great Famine, my father's imprisonment and exile to labor camps, the Cultural Revolution, and, perhaps most difficult of all, the inability for our family to get residence status, which meant that we would not receive any coupons to buy food, effectively banishing us to the countryside. Sometimes, she spoke as if something blocked her throat, and then she would suddenly stop herself.

As I grew older, the desire to learn more about my family's history grew stronger. During the course of writing this memoir, I often experienced heart-wrenching emotions as I revisited my childhood days, but my desire to find the missing and broken pieces of my family's history and put them back together kept me going. I needed to learn and understand this part of my life and my ancestor's lives, and I share it with you, dear reader, before the old generations are gone.

—AMY CHAN ZHOU

CHAPTER 1

MY GRANDPARENTS' LOVE

I WAS SENT TO THE COUNTRYSIDE to live with my maternal grandparents when I was only one year old. Their house was less than a half-mile away from a branch of the Pearl River in southern China. Tall levees were built along each side of the river; palm trees grew neatly on both sides of the levee. It was a beautiful, secluded spot. Connected by the river, a canal passed through my grandma's village like a silver belt. On each side of the canal there was a lot of bamboo. The small shoots were as big as a broomstick, and the big ones were as tall as a three-story building. Village houses lay along the canal. There were many ponds, large and small, next to the houses. As such, the village was like a water village. My grandparents' house was nearly surrounded by a huge pond. On the other side of the pond was a litchi orchard, which used to belong to my grandparents and later belonged to the People's Commune. Beyond the orchard there were miles of paddy fields.

The house had three bedrooms. I slept in my grandparents' room. The house was old, in bad shape, and built with mud and some small bricks, but it housed many pieces of beautiful, fancy furniture. The bed I slept in with my grandparents was a big redwood antique that had a roof. All the posts and legs were carved with dragons and clouds.

I still could not walk normally at age three because my bones were weak. I remember that Gong Gong (Grandpa) always brought me candy when he came home. Later, when he went out, I would block him by the door, so he would put me on his neck, and I grabbed his hair to hold on as we walked to the village. On a sunny day, Gong Gong would bring two antique hardwood chairs to a flat area in the yard. He sat on one chair, and Po Po (Grandma) would put me into the other chair. I could not sit or crawl on the ground because the bugs would bite my legs. I still remember watching little ants crawling in the gap of the bricks on the ground. . . . As time went on, my grandfather could not sit that way anymore because he got weak and then weaker. I saw him lying on a reclining lounge chair all the time. He enjoyed it when I rubbed and patted his legs with my little hands; I was proud I could make him happy.

Po Po, my maternal grandmother, was the center of my life. She had a kindly and amiable face with big eyes. Her hair was dark gray and tied in a knot. That made her show off two long ears that people admired very much because people believed long ears brought good luck and long life. Indeed, she always had very good health and was energetic. She also had a big light pink birthmark on her right cheek that people believed would bring prosperity, so she was always welcomed by all the village families. She was very wise, kind, caring, and generous to everybody. She taught her children never to argue with other people even if they were being unreasonable. She used to say: "If you are one-hundred percent right, you have to admit that you are only sixty percent right so you always leave some room for others. Arguing with others is always a losing game." One time I traveled with her to the next town. We saw a skinny beggar in front of a store; she took out 0.50 yuan and gave it to him. After we walked away, she said to me, "Aa Jade, when you grow up and have money, always give some to the people who need it."

I felt that I was very special to her. Po Po always saved the best stuff for me. She had two dozen grandchildren, but she brought only me whenever she visited relatives and friends. Sometimes, when I went out with her on the street, people came out to greet us and invited us into their homes. Then they usually asked Po Po for some advice on raising kids or about medicinal remedies to treat disease. Po Po always had answers. I remember she picked some wild grass whenever anyone got sick in the family. My happiest days were going out with her. She liked to visit her cousins in the town of Zhongshan, which was about eighteen kilometers from our home. She used to travel by getting free rides in passing vehicles since only a few buses went to town each day. Whenever she saw a vehicle passing by, she raised her arm, and then the drivers used to stop next to us because we were very old and very young. I have been in a truck full of pigs and chickens and even logs. Once we reached her cousin's home, we were always welcomed, then I would have a nice meal with a little meat. Normally, we didn't have any meat at home.

When I grew up, I recognized some inconsistencies in my grandparents' life: we lived in a poor house but had fancy furniture; we had a poor diet, but Po Po occasionally mentioned fancy foods that I had never seen. One day, Po Po pointed to the flat area in the yard I used to sit on and told me that it was the foundation of their original big house.

Before the new government came into power, my mother's parents used to own a lot of land, including many acres of paddy fields, two litchi orchards, a few fishponds, lotus ponds, and water chestnut ponds. Nonetheless, they were very low-key people; they worked very hard and never hired any maids or servants even though they had been quite well off. They hired seasonal workers to work in the paddy fields and the orchards. During the busy seasons, they had about ten workers. Every day there were two tables of people for lunch: one table for the family, and the other one for the workers.

During the time of war and turmoil, most wealthy families had guards. My grandparents did not have guards, which often made them the target of robbers. My grandparents had a big house on a peninsula that was nearly entirely surrounded by a huge pond. Since they were robbed several times, my grandparents expanded the pond to completely surround the house, so the house was on an island. They placed a small, removable, wooden bridge between the island and the main road. Every night, they pulled the wooden bridge away with a rope and landed their boats on the island to prevent thieves from crossing over.

I never felt that my life was miserable in the countryside since I grew up there without knowing the outside world. Once I could walk and run, I would not stay at home and ran around everywhere in the village.

My hard of hearing, mute uncle was never married and lived in my grandma's house. He was very handy. He liked to use bamboo to make baskets, furniture, and other items. He treated me like his daughter, and I could make him do anything for me. He made all kinds of gestures in front of me, but a lot of times I had no idea what he meant. I often did stupid things, such as pulling out a flower in the yard, playing with mud, and getting into the duck's cage, making my clothes all dirty. One time, my hard of hearing uncle drew a picture of a stamp on a small piece of paper, put the "stamp" on my forehead, and pointed in the direction out of our village with the "Ne, Ne!" noise he made.

I understood that he meant if I did not behave, he would drop me at the post office to send me back to my mother.

As I got older, there never seemed to be enough food, so I was always hungry. Our main food was rice and vegetables, and occasionally, we had some dried salt fish. Lacking nutrition, I looked for food all the time in the wild countryside. There were many sugarcane fields along the river since the ground was blessed with rich, fertile soil. Sometimes I followed the older kids to get inside the field and fill up my stomach with sugarcane juice. Although the sugarcane field belonged to the commune, in my young mind, I only knew what was edible or inedible. Since I rarely ate meat, the bamboo worm was a delicacy for me because it was full of oil. Oil was scarce because all locally produced peanut oil had to be sent to the government and distributed to the cities or exported to Hong Kong. In the spring, when the bamboo shoots started to explode from the ground vertically into columns, they grew fast, up to three feet a day. I would pay attention to the tips of the shoots to see if there was a worm inside. When I spotted a bamboo shoot that had a small hole on it, I knew there was a worm in it. Getting a worm from a big bamboo shoot was not easy since it was so tall. The worm almost always lived and grew at the tip of the bamboo shoot. One day I spotted a bamboo shoot with a hole and tried very hard to shake it free. A few boys in the village saw me and came to help.

"Go away! I do not want your help."

I knew they wanted me to share the bamboo worm. They persisted so they could get their share. A few of us yanked the bamboo very hard left and right, putting all our body weight into it. Finally, the bamboo broke. I picked up the big fat yellow worm, about two inches long, which looked like a big fat finger. Then I ran to my kitchen and fried it in a wok. The boys followed me. After the worm browned, I cut it into a few pieces, and each of us would eat one small piece. It was yummy for us because it was creamy and oily. The adults did not like us doing that because we ruined a bamboo shoot for just one worm.

Catching bamboo worms was a challenge, but getting bee worms was a big adventure. The yellow bee worms (bee pupae) from a beehive were also a delicacy. They were as tasty as the bamboo worms. Acquiring them was dangerous, but one beehive might have at least a dozen worms. Whenever we spotted a beehive, our stomachs gurgled and our saliva dripped in anticipation. One day during a hot summer, the air evaporated from the ground; I walked with my cousin, Ruen. He was almost three years old than I. The sunbaked road was so hot we hopped and ran with our bare feet. When we stopped under a palm tree to cool down our feet, we spotted a few hornets flying around under a small palm tree; we immediately knew that there had to be a beehive under there.

Ruen said, "See the honeycomb there? Let's get it!"

"Noooo," I replied.

"Coward. I'll go get it."

Coward was not a word I wanted to hear. I followed behind Ruen and walked toward the small palm tree.

"Wow! It's a big nest," we both observed.

He grabbed a small stick from the ground and used it to poke at the nest. Suddenly, a swarm of bees flew out. I yelled, "Be careful!" then ran away as fast as I could. I looked back; I saw a large army of bees flying after my cousin. I was so scared my heart almost jumped out of my body. Within a few seconds, Ruen ran ahead of me because he was big and older than I was. I thought the bees would sting me, so I vigorously flapped both of my hands.

Surprisingly, the bees knew who had attacked their nest; they passed right by me and continued to chase Ruen. He covered his head with his hands and suddenly jumped into a pound he had run by.

I ran to the edge of the pound and yelled: "Ruen! Are you okay?"

His hair emerged out of the water, his hands still scratching his head. Later, he came up to the bank and stood in front of me like a wet log. He looked at me and did not talk at all. He must have been stung by two dozen bees. His face and ears immediately swelled up, making him look like a fat pig. His eyes became thin lines.

I kept asking, "Are you okay?"

He did not say anything because he was in great pain. I think jumping into the water probably saved his life because there were so many bees following him. After this, we should have never tried to touch the beehives again. But when we spotted beehives again, we could not resist the creamy taste of bee worms, and so we would take the risk yet another time.

CHAPTER 2

MY MOTHER AND MY FATHER

MY MOTHER WAS BORN IN 1939 in the village of Zhong-shan, as the oldest daughter and the sixth child in the family. She had six brothers, five of whom were older than she, and three sisters. Two of her brothers died during the Japanese invasion. (See Appendix B.)

During World War II, Japanese soldiers were chasing two girls from a neighboring village; they wanted to catch and rape them. However, the two girls ran into my grandma's village and hid there. The Japanese soldiers then set fire to the village. My mother's family left their house to escape from the Japanese. The fifth brother fell and broke a bone in his back while escaping. My grandmother could not bring him to the hospital on time so the bone healed in the wrong position. He suffered from severe pain and later died just before his high school graduation.

After the Japanese burned down the village, the family came back home and found that their big house was destroyed by fire. My grandmother carried her youngest toddler son on her back and searched for her gold jewelry under the ash. She needed those things badly to get money to rebuild the house. Unfortunately, the child on her back inhaled a lot of smoke and ash; he died within a few days. The value of her burned-down jewelry would only cover building a small house. As a result, the whole family lived in a smaller house after that.

As the oldest daughter in the family, my mother had many responsibilities. She helped my grandmother do all the chores. During the times of seeding and the harvest season, she brought the workers to work at the orchards or the paddy fields when she was only nine years old. That was because her older brothers all went to school. In old China, people considered that education was important for men but less important for women. Since the family lost their wealth during the Japanese invasion, my grandparents did not let my mother go to school. These days my mother still blames her parents for not letting her attend school.

During the Land Reform Movement (see Appendix A-1), the new government took over all my grandparents' land properties overnight. The big shock caused my mother's grandmother to have a mental breakdown. She became a maniac; day and night, she went repeatedly to a huge levee that was about thirty feet high. She stood on top of the levee to see if anybody was coming to the village and ran back furiously to the village yelling, "They are coming! They are coming! The communists are coming!" pointing her finger toward the entrance of the village. At first, my grandfather tried to lock her in the house, but it became too hard for him to lock away his sick mother. He eventually let her run out again. One night, she went to the levee, and on the way back to the village, while crossing a small, single-log wooden bridge, she fell into the water and drowned. After my great-grandmother died, some of the village people claimed that they saw an old woman running and crying in the village at night. They thought it was the ghost of my great-grandmother. This caused fear in the village, and people would not go out at night. They were superstitious; they believed that dead people usually wandered around in this world if they had worries unresolved during their lifetime. The people in the village requested that my grandparents hire Buddhist monks to pray and guide the ghost to leave the village and go to heaven. Villagers were relieved after the monks chanted; they started to go out again at night. However, one night a woman walked out and heard the wind blow in a bamboo forest near the single-log wooden bridge; she yelled, "The ghost is weeping! Listen, she refuses to leave." Hearing the ghastly and blood-curdling wailing, people ran back to their houses. The next day, rumors of a ghost woman crying spread through the entire village again. Some of them even claimed that they saw a shadow on the bridge. The villagers wanted my grandfather to hire the monks again. Subsequently, my grandfather had to pay the monks to try a second time to calm his mother's spirit and invite her to leave the earth. . . .

A "father" was an imaginary figure in my childhood because my father left us when I was about one year old. I grew up without his presence throughout my childhood. When I first realized all the children in the village had a father, I started to question, "Who is my father? Where is my father?" When I asked my mother, she did not give me an answer. Instead, she gave me a very sad look. As a very young, innocent child, I quickly accepted the fact that I did not have a father. Since I never saw my father, I did not feel that I missed him. However, I heard some bits and pieces of stories about my father's relatives when I grew up.

One day, while I was cleaning vegetables in a canal next to my house, a young man, a stranger, came to me and asked, "Child, do you know Zhen?"

I looked at him; he seemed to come from far away because his accent was so different from our local one. I realized that this guy was looking for my mother. I immediately became alert because my maternal grandmother Po Po told me all time to "never tell a stranger where we live." She told me that bad people from far away could come and arrest the local people. The man stood and waited for an answer, so I pointed to the house that my grandmother lived in.

"I don't know. You may ask an old lady who lives in that house."

The man walked to the house and called out, "Hello, anybody at home?"

Po Po came out and was surprised. "Yinsheng, is that you? You grew up into a big man!"

Then my grandmother pointed at me and told him: "She is your uncle's daughter, Ah Jade."

Then she said to me, "Ah Jade, this is your cousin, come and greet him."

They walked into the house and continued their discussion.

I stayed outside but overheard some conversation. "My Nai Nai [paternal grandmother] asked where my uncle is . . ." came from my cousin, and Po Po said, "Your uncle is in . . ."

This was the first time I saw a relative from my father's side and realized that my father was still alive! My desire to find out more about him became stronger.

My father was born in December 1931 in Gaozhou, Guangdong, the third child in the family. He had an older brother who died during the Great Famine around 1960, a younger brother, and two sisters. The youngest sister was given up for adoption during the Great Famine; they didn't have enough food to feed her.

My paternal grandfather, Zebang Chen, was a traditional private teacher in a warlord's, Chen Jitang's, family.

When China's first democratic republic failed, civil wars broke out between more than a dozen warlords. After years of conflict with Chiang Kai-shek, who was the head of the Kuomintang's army and later became the president of China—the Kuomintang was the ruling party that was defeated by the communists and then settled in Taiwan— Chen Jitang lost and settled down in Hong Kong. He asked my grandfather to go with him, but my grandfather decided to stay. Grandpa died early, leaving five children and his wife.

My grandfather had two older brothers; the oldest brother, Fenggao Chen, was a judge in Guangzhou City. (See Appendix B.) During the Japanese invasion in World War II, granduncle Fenggao attempted to escape from the city while the Japanese were coming. Unfortunately, he and his son, on their way to their countryside home, were killed by the bombardment of Japanese warplanes.

The second brother of my grandfather, Weiqun Chen, was a doctor of traditional Chinese medicine who owned an herbal medicine clinic. (See Appendix B.) He also managed the family's farmland in the countryside. After my grandfather's death, as tradition dictated, he took care of my grandfather's family and their share of land since he was the oldest man in the family. From that day on, my father and his uncle's children treated each other like brothers and sisters, not cousins. My father helped in the busy clinic. Many years later in my life, my father told me many stories about his youth: "Sometimes there were so many patients waiting in the clinic that your granduncle had to skip lunch. By helping him, I slowly learned some Chinese herbal medicine and weighed it for the patients." My granduncle liked my father because he was smart, hardworking, and was a top student in school. He even treated my father better than his own children. My father told me: "Once your granduncle bought a wool coat for me as a reward for my good grades, but not for any of his biological children because they did so poorly in school."

Since my father was a bright and hardworking student, my granduncle sent him to an expensive western-style high school founded by the British. The school required the students to speak English. After my father graduated from high school, he was admitted to a college in Guangzhou in 1950. In the old days, going to college was considered very prestigious. Our family had an educational foundation created by Chen's ancestors for anyone in the family who was accepted to college. The foundation provided 1,200 pounds of grain to encourage the younger generation to study hard. My father was the only one who got into college. Everyone in the family and the county were proud of him because only three students got into college from their county that year. Unfortunately, our family's educational foundation was lost with the change in the government. My father did not receive anything from the foundation, but my granduncle financially supported him in college.

My father graduated from college. He should have had a bright future waiting for him because a college degree was rare at that time; but times had changed in China. After eight years of the Japanese invasion and three years of civil war, the communists took over China in 1949. Like most Chinese people who desperately hoped for peace and a better life, my father believed in the new government.

The new communist government undertook a massive economic and social reconstruction effort in China to rebuild war-damaged industries and restore the crippled economy. These efforts were welcomed by the Chinese people, who enthusiastically responded to the rebuilding of China. But the government also launched many political movements. As a result, there was great turmoil created. Like millions of Chinese people, my father's dramatic life journey had just begun.

After graduating from college, my father found his first job as a branch chief in Xingning county government in the Guangdong province. For a young man, this was a great job. He prided himself on working very hard and was very enthusiastic about building a new country just like the other citizens were.

A short time later, the government started the "Suppress Counter-revolutionaries" campaign. (See Appendix A-2.) This effort was to crack down on the few remaining opposition movements to the communist government and on spies from the Kuomintang party as well as from foreign countries. The campaign movement was expanded, and it escalated. As a result, most people from a formerly rich family were being investigated for any ties with the former government or foreign countries.

My granduncle Weiqun, who took care of my father, was under investigation. He was interrogated by the local village leaders and activists for days and nights without sleep. They wanted him to confess what he and his family members had done in the old China. At first, he didn't give any information under pressure, no matter how they tortured him, since he had no real ties with the old government. Later they used a metal chain to tie his feet and hang him from a tree upside down. As a doctor, he knew what would happen to him if they continued to hang him even a little bit longer. He gave in under this cruel torture simply because physical suffering had weakened his willpower. He confessed that my father joined "The Youth of the Three People Principles" league. The Three People Principle (Nationalism, Democracy, and the People's Livelihood) was Dr. Sun Yatsen's, the founding father of the Republic of China, vision for China. The league was created by the Kuomintang party for young students to pursue Sun Yatsen's ideology. Then the activists traveled to my father's workplace to investigate him. They scrutinized his family and investigated what he had done when he was in high school. They also found out that his high school was founded by the British. The activists usually had very little education. They considered that anyone who had contact with the western world must be a western spy. The government office immediately expelled my father from his branch chief position and sent him to jail for almost three years. During those three years, no one knew where he was because he was not allowed to contact anyone, not even his family.

Since that time, my father was thrown into a bottomless chasm of dreadful events. The leaders in the village changed my grandmother's status from middle-class peasant to landlord. My grandmother was heartbroken that her brother-in-law, whom she trusted so much, would betray her. However, my father never blamed his uncle, who was forced to provide the information. He was always grateful that his uncle raised him as his own child and supported his education from high school to college.

My father was released from jail in 1957 and went to his oldest cousin Guishen's home in Guangzhou City. Guishen opened the door with surprise to see how scruffy looking my father was. Looking at the sallow and emaciated man, she asked my father, "What happened? You have a college degree and a branch chief position. How could you become like this?" My father told her how he spent three miserable years in jail. But he did not tell her it was because of her father who had betrayed him.

Because of my father's history in the old society, his future was ruined. After my father got out of jail, he refused to go back to his hometown to become a peasant. He knew that with his record, it would be very hard for him to live there. It was also difficult for him to stay in the city because his residence register was revoked from the city and placed back in his hometown of Gaozhou. Luckily, Guishen's husband Zhongbao was a judge in Guangzhou City. He helped my father change his name and transferred the residence register back to Guangzhou City. From then on, my father's name was Rong Chen.

CHAPTER 3

THE FATE OF BEING LABELED LANDLORD CLASS

THE COMMUNIST THEORY of "class struggle" was practiced in China. Mao Zedong wrote an article, "Analyzing
Each Social Class in Chinese Society," in 1925, that classified the different social classes in China. This became the
theory that guided the communist party in defining their
base as well as their enemies in China. Mao led the earlier
revolution by the Land Reform Movement in the countryside in the late 1920s. The Land Reform Movement spread
continuously until the early 1950s after the communists
had taken over the government. According to that article,
farmers were classified into different categories: landlords, rich peasants, middle-class peasants, lower-middle-class peasants, and poor peasants. The farm owners
were referred to as "landlords" in China. The landlords
were treated like counter-revolutionaries and public enemies, and the poor peasants became the "masters of
the country." During this movement, the government (or
Peasant Union before the communists replaced the existing government) took over the ownership of land owned
by the landlords.

People who had been classified as "landlords" were
now a shamed group of people in society. Unfortunately, my granduncle Weiqun's family's status was "landlord." All his land was confiscated; the family's herbal
medicine clinic became state-owned, and even his house
and my paternal grandmother Nai Nai's house, were distributed to others. However, my Nai Nai's family status

was determined to be a "middle-class peasant" because she gave all the rights to her husband's brother after my grandfather's death. Unfortunately, my Nai Nai's status from the middle class was changed to landlord in the later political movement.

On my mother's side of the family, my grandparents were first classified in the landlord category according to the amount of land they owned. My grandfather requested to change his status because he had a small house, and he never hired any servants or permanent workers. As a result, the local leader changed his category from "landlord" to "middle-class peasant."

The Land Reform Movement (see Appendix A-1) took away land from the landlords, and there were also many "Public Accusation and Denouncing Meetings" in those days to physically and mentally abuse the landlords in public and even kill them after the meeting without due process in court. During one such meeting, the militants pulled out all the landlords from different areas and sent them to a stage. All of them were tied up, and each of them had a sign reading I AM GUILTY hanging from their neck. The public accusation meetings started with a few indignant poor peasants who accused the landlords of exploiting the peasants during the old society. When the meeting reached its climax, a person shouted with a loudspeaker: "Down with the landlords!" and "Shoot them!" Then the audience echoed the sentiment.

My maternal grandma, Po Po, had a neighbor who was a landlord. He joined the Kuomintang before the communists took over China. When he and other landlords were paraded in the village before being executed in public, some of the villagers closed their windows and hid in their houses. Old people believed those landlords' souls were already detached from their bodies before they died. Their souls might try to attach to a shadow of clothing hanging to dry. Fearing this, Po Po immediately picked up the clothing from the bamboo sticks and went into the house. After a few gunshots, her landlord neighbor collapsed to the ground. His older son went to pick up his father's body. Looking at his father lying down full of blood, terror stabbed his heart, and his body shook with fear. Later, the son became deranged. He died within a year, leaving behind his wife and two daughters. His wife left her children and remarried to avoid the title of landlord class. The two girls were my schoolmates. Unfortunately, they dropped out of school at the end of the semester in the first grade, and we did not know what happened to them after that.

There was a "haunted," sun-dried field in the village. I used to avoid going there or ran as fast as I could to pass it after dark because people said there were ghosts there. My aunt told me that there was a big mansion including many houses in that field that belonged to the biggest landlord in our village. During the Land Reform Movement, the old landlord was executed, and his young wife and children were kicked out of the houses. The houses were distributed to multiple families of poor peasants. One day, the houses caught on fire. Many soldiers from the local liberation army troop came to help put out the fire. Unfortunately, a man was killed by the fire, and the houses were burned down. After that, rumors spread in the village. People thought the ghost of the old landlord had come back for revenge; bad things happened to the poor families that lived there. One day, the local leader and activists set up a public accusation meeting against the landlord's surviving widow. They dragged her by her hair, pulled her on the stage, and accused her of using some kind of voo-doo tricks to invite the ghosts to burn down the houses and sabotage the new socialist society. After the meeting, they poured concrete on top of the foundation of the burned-down mansion to make a grain-drying field and stop the ghosts from coming out of the ground. This was so stu-pid and contradicted the communists' atheistic ideology, which is against the belief in any god or ghost. It clearly showed that the grassroots activists at that time were ig-norant and uneducated. They were self-proclaimed com-munists, but they had no clue what communism was.

After the Land Reform Movement, the government launched another movement, the "Campaign to Suppress Counter-revolutionaries" (see Appendix A-2) in the ear-ly 1950s. This caused my father to go to jail. Besides, my fourth aunt-in-law was from a landlord's family, and her older brother was a member of the Kuomintang party. When I was a kid, I often heard the village women gossip and call my aunt-in-law a "shot-dead ghost's daughter." It was because both her father and brother were executed.

My family's tragedy was just beginning. It was the epitome of thousands of landlords suffering in Chinese society during that time. Their lives were shattered just because they were born into landlords' families.

Chapter 4

FROM THE "GREAT LEAP FORWARD" TO THE "GREAT FAMINE"

THE GOAL OF THE GREAT LEAP FORWARD Movement (see Appendix A-5) was to boost China's economy by escalating industrial and agriculture production. The intentions of the young communist government were good. Mao announced the goal of surpassing the steel production output of Great Britain in fifteen years' time. At the same time, Mao also wanted to accomplish a transformation to a Marxist communist society. He directed the formation of People's Communes in the countryside by recombining all the land that had been distributed previously to the lower-class peasants. This ended the private ownership of land in China. All land and production equipment became public property. Each village became a production team under a People's Commune where people would eat and work together. "Public Canteens" were created for the entire village to eat together.

Everyone in my maternal grandparents' village was herded together to eliminate private ownership. People could not keep their livestock, their grain, their tools, even their cookware at home. In the beginning, the village people tried to hide their possessions. My grandparents feared there would be negative consequences if everyone ate together. They placed their grain under a big tree in the same hole in which my grandparents had hidden grain during the Japanese invasion. Unfortunately, some children playing a scavenger hunt found out there was some grain hidden under the tree. They told some adults who then reported it to the village leaders; therefore, my grandparents' grain was confiscated by the commune.

All this happened from 1958 to 1962 before I was born, but I heard many stories about it from an old "big mouthed" lady who liked to tell old stories to young kids like us. The children called her "Ah Po." She used to brag, "Kids, I eat salt more than you eat rice." We all looked at her curiously. I asked her: "Why couldn't you cook and eat at home at that time?" She said, "To eat at home? The cadres patrolled the streets, looked for smoke from the chimney of the houses. If they caught you hiding food at home, they made you parade in the street with a dunce hat on!" The dunce hat was a cylindrical pig's cage made from bamboo that was used to bring pigs to sell in the market, then covered with cone-shaped white paper to put on somebody's head for the purpose of humiliation. As a consequence, villagers didn't dare to hide anything. Some of them even handed out their family's treasures, like wedding rings, jewelry, and antiques. Anything edible, they would just try to eat as much as they could.

The public canteen was for the whole village to eat together in buffet style every day. At the beginning of the mass communal eating, the animals also had a good time. Because there was so much leftover food and tremendous waste, food that would have fed a village for a season vanished in a month; the leftovers were fed to the dogs and pigs. Of course, their good time did not last long. When the food became insufficient, people killed all those animals, even pets, to eat.

Upping steel production was also a big plan. In order to rapidly raising industrial production, the peasants were also directed to devote all their energy to making steel, some of the villages leaving spring farming unattended. How did they make steel? People simply set up home-made furnaces everywhere, flames lighting up the sky. My grandparents' village did not build any amateur furnaces, but they were required to send a few strong laborers to another production team that had furnaces. The local leaders sent people from house to house to collect pots and pans, anything that was made from metal to melt in the furnace. So it was not real steel production from iron ore, but used existing metal to melt it instead. My father told us that there was a fire station in Guangzhou City, which had an automatic steel door. When the fire truck drove out, the iron door automatically opened. People took out the door and threw it into the furnace, and a useless steel ball came out. My father knew that would harm the country more than benefit it. He even predicted in front of his employees that the blind action would result in disaster.

The local cadres were under a lot of pressure from the high authorities, and they wanted to satisfy the target production number that was assigned to them. But those numbers were not realistic, so they forced the peasants to fake the numbers, saying that their land could produce a few times more grain than the years before. In those days when people read the newspaper, there were reports about how production teams had reached more than 100,000 pounds of grain on one "Mu" of land, which is about 0.164 acres. My father said that anybody who had a brain would not believe it. This prompted people to lie and accept fake reports without facts. When lies replaced the truth in society, it would have horrible consequences later. The true story was that the production team gathered grain from many acres of the land and piled it up into one acre so that they could get credit from the government for the large amount. They were glorified for a moment, but they were the first to suffer hunger at the end. This was because the government would take more grain away since the local leaders reported much more than the actual amount of production. Some villages ended up handing away all their production and could not even keep any seeds. There was nothing left to feed the peasants. This situation, along with the wastage of food in the public canteen, soon led to a scarcity of food, and the people started to suffer from hunger. Ah Po once said, "A leader in the next village committed suicide because he felt guilty for faking the number of the harvest." As a result, there were millions of deaths from starvation.

The first ones to die of hunger in our villages were the landlords or those who had been identified as "bad elements" because they got less food allotment. My grandmother did not see her neighbor go out for a few weeks, and she worried about her because her family was landlord class. My grandmother brought a half bowl of rice and checked on her; she found out the lady of the house did not have pants to wear because she used her only pants in exchange for food. By the time my grandmother saw her, she had lain on her bed with a sheet covered up her legs. Her feet were swollen due to hunger. People who survived after the Great Leap Forward movement were severely malnourished.

Ah Po and other villagers sometimes mentioned their experiences with hunger. They called the time of "Four Liang a Day." That meant that each villager only had four "Liang" of rice per day. One Liang is about 1.6 ounces. When they talked about Four Liang, none of them would blame the government. They had been told that the shortage of food was caused by natural disaster, and the Soviets, who demanded China pay back their loan. The Soviet Union had supported the young Chinese communist government with industrial machinery. When the relationship severed, the Soviets asked the Chinese government to pay them back for the machinery. My aunt told me that each of the working laborers in the village got four Liang of grain a day during that time; a non-working adult got two Liang of grain; a child got one Liang at that time. There was no meat and no other non-staple food. Luckily, my grandparents' home was close to a canal, a river, so they survived the famine by fishing. Nonetheless, there were still about seventy deaths during the Great Famine in our surrounding area, according to my grandmother's count.

My father's hometown, Gaozhou, was much worse than my mother's hometown because it was in a mountain area, the transportation was not good, and access to drinking water was not easy for them. Each day the village people had to carry water from the bottom of the mountain to cook. Imagine how difficult it was to grow food. During the Great Famine, hunger was unavoidable, and people did not even have the strength to carry their water. My father's older brother died due to a lack of food, and he left his wife with two young children. From that day on, my father took care of his older brother's family just as his uncle did for him. Once in desperation, my grandmother Nai Nai went to Granduncle Weiqun's home and asked if she could borrow a cup of rice so she could make porridge for her children. She thought my granduncle might be better off than she because he was at least a well-known doctor. Even though he was a good doctor, he was also considered an evil landlord. He did not have food to give to her. In the end, my grandmother did not want the whole family to die together, so she gave her youngest daughter away for adoption.

My father's youngest sister Guijuan was the unluckiest person in the family. She was born into a landlord's family and had not enjoyed a day of wealthy life but carried the stigma of a bad title into the new regime. Her father died when she was very young. By the time she could enter school, the family was too poor to send her. My grandmother reluctantly gave her to a family that had no children when she was around fourteen years old. That family believed a girl was good luck and could bring a little brother to the family. Four years later, a skinny young girl came into the house. My grandmother Nai Nai recognized her daughter and learned how harshly the adoptive family treated her daughter after they gave birth to a boy. My grandmother Nai Nai was hoping her daughter could marry a man who had enough food to feed her. So they let her marry a young man who lived in a place that was located on the border of Macau. The husband's job was as a "people's guard" meant to catch the people who attempted to escape to Macau. After marriage, he forbade his wife to visit her mother because he did not want her family's landlord title to ruin his job. As a result, Guijuan did not have a chance to see her mother again after she married.

The "Great Leap Forward" became "The Great Famine." There was a severe shortage of food and products like fabric, soap, and more throughout the entire country. Consequently, the government started to control the food and the distribution of essential living materials. For that, the government issued a new policy that each citizen had to register for a residence permit in their local jurisdiction. A registered city resident would be issued a monthly allowance of a limited amount of food-purchasing coupons. Without the registration of the city, they would not be able to get the coupons. In the countryside, limited grain was distributed to each registered household from their production team (one village formed one production team).

CHAPTER 5

MY FATHER MEETS MY MOTHER

ALTHOUGH MY FATHER WENT BACK to Guangzhou City after jail and became a resident in the city, he did not dare to take a job in the government or state-owned companies. He declined an engineering position from a government division, which offered him ninety-nine yuan per month. At that time, an average worker in the city only earned around twenty-five yuan per month. Because he was worried that the government agency might find out about his background again, he decided to work for himself as a construction contractor to be safe. In the beginning, the new communist government still allowed a small percentage of people to work for themselves as small business owners. He had a reputation for honesty, intelligence, generosity, and respecting others. Therefore, he always had a lot of friends and connections and his business boomed.

My mother also lived in Guangzhou City at that time. Since my mother was very capable of taking care of the family farm, my grandparents took her everywhere with them to buy and sell items in the city. Once, while they were visiting a relative, who was a single old woman in Guangzhou City, that relative liked my mother so much that she asked my grandmother to allow her daughter to stay with her in the city. She said to my grandmother, "Oh, your daughter is lovely, you have so many children, can she stay with me? I will treat her like my own daughter—of course, she is always your daughter." My grandmother let my mother decide. My mother chose to stay in the city, so she settled in the city in 1953 when she was only about fourteen years old. From that time, she started to work in the city doing various jobs.

One day my father went to his friend's jobsite and saw a beautiful, curly-haired-girl who was talking to his friend. Her teeth were perfectly straight and sparkled like white pearls. That was my mother. My father was shocked and immediately attracted to this young woman, so he went to talk to his friend. He asked, "Who is this girl? Where did she come from?" His friend told him that she was working for him.

My father asked his friend for a favor. He said, "I want to date her. Can you fire her and recommend her to my company, then she can work for me?" So his friend did just that. She became a cook in my father's company. My mother still could remember vividly that when she was working for my father, every time she had some questions to ask my father, all the other employees walked away from them. When she went home, all the other employees were reluctant to give her a ride. In the end, there was only my father who was willing to give her a ride. That was a planned trick; everybody in the company tried to get them together. When my father proposed, my mother refused him. She told him that she was uneducated and only had gone to school for a short time. He was skeptical and took my mother to visit his younger cousin Guijing and asked her to see if his new girlfriend was educated or not. During the visit, Guijing was measuring a piece of fabric and making a two-piece dress for her daughter. A girl was playing with a doll next to her. My mother stood next to them and watched quietly as Guijing measured the fabric a few times, saying, "Not enough fabric; the kid is growing fast." My mother said, "You have enough. You should cut this corner and make a collar; the big pieces are going to be an upper shirt and a skirt. The rest of it is going to make sleeves." Guijing asked my mother to do the cutting. There was still a little fabric left. She said, "You can use this to make two strings to hold the skirt. Your girl will look like an angel." After the pieces were cut, my mother helped Guijing sew them. Within a short time, the beautiful two-piece set was finished. The girl tried them on; they were perfect on her.

After that, Guijing told my father, "Your girlfriend is an educated woman; she is so smart. Her conversation is elegant, and she must be from a very good family."

"Why does she lie to me?" my father asked.

Guijing said: "The reason is simply that she wanted to reject you without hurting you."

My father believed in his soul that he loved this girl. He bought a big gold necklace for my mother as an engagement gift. My mother refused to accept it. Later, my mother could not resist the love of my father, and she went to ask her father for advice. Her father told her, "Go marry him," and "Don't come back home because we have a food shortage in the countryside." It was the time of the Great Leap Forward Movement, which was later followed by the Great Famine. It was the most devastating catastrophe in recent history in China. My father was one of the few people who did not suffer because he was a contractor and made enough money to buy food from the black market.

My mother finally married my father in 1959. Was this because of a coincidence? Destiny? From then their fates were tied together. Every time my father mentioned how he met my mother, he was very proud and dreamed about the sweetness of that time.

CHAPTER 6

ENDLESS POLITICAL CAMPAIGNS: PEOPLE AGAINST PEOPLE

FROM THE EARLY 1950S, the government initiated many political campaigns (see Appendix A 1-5); it was a continuous effort against all who were not in line with the "communist doctrine." In each of the political movements, there was always an expansion for a targeted group of people who would become class enemies. It promoted hatred in society. The authorities encouraged people to be informers to mutually disclose each other's personal history, background, even current daily activities, lifestyle, and more. One of the ugliest parts was that the local officials demanded everybody be an informer to report the actions of their family members and friends. Such practices turned people against each other and profoundly destroyed human relationships and social trust. There was fear in society. The proliferation of the government's movements made more victims from innocent citizens.

It was in 1962. My parents lived in Guangzhou City. They rented an apartment at #2 Guan-Yuan Street in a Victorian-style house built by an American doctor. The house had a big porch in front and a huge garden behind the house. My parents lived on the first floor. The landlord was a young lady who lived on the second floor. Her father was a friend of the American owner, and they both had left China during the civil war. My father took very good care of the garden because he liked flowers very much so the garden proliferated with different kinds of flowers year-round—the unique Victorian-style house was stunningly beautiful in the crowded city. Next door lived a middle-aged couple, the Yangs. They used to live in Singapore before communists took over China; they came back because Mr. Yang had a health problem that he could not find a cure for in Singapore. He came back to search for alternate care, and luckily, a traditional Chinese doctor was able to cure his problem, then he decided to settle down in China. The wife was a very affectionate person with a warm personality. When my mother had my older sister, she offered to bathe my sister every evening. On the other hand, Mr. Yang was a quiet man and always had a gentle smile. He was a business owner but became an ordinary worker in the new government. Even as an ordinary worker, a businessman always had a business vision no matter in what environment. Mr. Yang saw that the peasants worked very hard to carry human and animal waste to the field as fertilizer, so he got an idea of selling chemical fertilizer to the farmers. In those days, there was a shortage of chemical fertilizers in China. Mr. Yang asked his brother, who lived in Singapore, to send him small amounts of fertilizer that he sold to the farmers. This import and trade was illegal at that time. One night, he was arrested by the authorities. He was found guilty of illegal trafficking of goods from a foreign country. All the neighbors tried to find out about his whereabouts and situation while he was in confinement. His wife was gravely worried about him and cried every day. Within a few weeks, he was badly beaten and returned home on a stretcher. His wife shed tears, and the neighbors ran out and wanted to help. My parents cooked for them, comforted them, and told them that everything would be fine. Mr. Yang, however, avoided eye contact with my father. My father thought he probably was too tired and didn't feel like talking about it.

One night after Mr. Yang came back home for a few days, my parents heard some rapid footsteps, and their doorbell rang repeatedly. My parents opened the door and saw about ten men and women. One was holding a pair of handcuffs, and another was holding a sheet of paper and announced that my father was guilty of "capitalist exploitation activity." They then rushed into the house and handcuffed my father. The others proceeded to vandalize the house and took everything they considered valuable. "No, no, don't break them," my mother said of her possessions. A ferocious guard stared at her and said, "You live a capitalist style of life." My sister sensed something was very wrong, so she ran to my mother and cringed behind her legs. My mother was petrified with terror. She watched my father being pushed out of the house; tears filled her eyes. Speechless, she was unable to comprehend what had just occurred. She cried bitterly with her daughter.

When Mr. Yang was in confinement, he was relentlessly interrogated by the government-appointed campaign activists. They took turns exerting pressure on him without allowing him to sleep. They wanted him to report other people who were suspicious and had any involvement related to "capitalism." This physical torture and poor diet caused him not to be able to walk. He could not stand the torture anymore, and finally, he reported that my father had a lot of friends gathering to eat dinner at night. Those activists thought they had discovered golden information. The report of a little bit of my father's private life had been elevated to an indictment of "capitalist corruption." Then they arrested my father for interrogation. They accused my father of gathering many people and eating all the time at night, which was a capitalist way of life, so he needed to be re-educated. The truth was my father had many guests after dinner; those people were his employees, and they brought their friends or relatives over in the hope that my father would hire them. With the conviction, my father was sent to a hard labor correction camp for "socialism re-education."

The Yangs felt embarrassed whenever they saw my parents. They felt guilty. But my father never blamed Mr. Yang for his arrest.

Chapter 7

"RE-EDUCATION" IN LABOR CAMPS

WHEN MY MOTHER WAS PREGNANT with me in 1964, my father had already undergone re-education in a labor correction camp. There, an administrative unit assigned him to live in a specific location where he worked, which was strictly supervised by correction officers. In the beginning, the local police ("Gong An") told my father that he would have to go there for a half year to be re-educated. They still paid my father a salary of fifteen yuan per month in the labor camp. In the early sixties in Guangzhou, China, a pound of pork with a rational coupon was around 1.7 yuan, but without a coupon it was twelve yuan per pound in the black market. My father did not get any coupons in the camp. Therefore, his whole month salary could barely buy a pound of pork.

The guards in the labor camp were insufferably arrogant. They would insult the workers at any time, even beat them. Most of the workers were scholars, landlords, small merchant traders, or so-called "capitalist roaders," former government officials who didn't follow Mao's directions to eliminate all private ownership. A few of the workers were communist leaders whose ideology was not in line with the political campaign. To avoid beatings, they put on faces and did not have the nerve to say a word. Anyone who did not please the guards would easily have a few more years in the camp added. The guards could set up public criticizing and denouncing meetings at any time for those who had not "behaved."

Everybody in the camp was extremely hungry due to the intense daily labor and the lack of food. From morning to night, their stomachs rumbled. The illusions of food and freedom were their hope for surviving. After a day of work, they were required to learn "Mao Zedong's thoughts," but with their dizzy heads and shaky legs from hunger, they just wanted to sit still to conserve their energy. They had no vigor to do much, but when the guards smoked outside of the house, all the laborers rushed to the window and tried to breathe in the smoke. Any smell, even smoke, would stimulate their nerves.

The situation in the labor camp was getting worse, and my father was hungry all the time, but he thought of his family first. He sacrificed himself and did not forget to send five yuans to his wife from his fifteen yuan salary. My father knew that my mother had a very difficult time at home since she had no right to work and to get coupons because of not having a resident permit.

Some of the workers, such as my father, had a little salary and could even go home to visit occasionally, but some could not, and it all depended on what "crime" they committed. My mother's oldest brother, I called him Big Uncle, was also in the labor camp in Zhongshan. Because he was charged with the crime of "speculation of profiteering trade," he had no salary and could not ever go home to visit. Even so, during his term in the labor camp, my grandmother sent her daughter to bring food to him. Some of the laborers were not fortunate enough to have family members visit or bring food. Big Uncle painfully told his family how his roommate died. One evening, his roommate told him, "I can't tolerate the hunger anymore. You are very lucky. Your family brings food to you." My uncle told him that if his sister brought food again, he would share a little with him. The next evening, my uncle walked to a pond and saw his roommate. My uncle walked close to him and found him swallowing sand and water. The man died the next day. These kinds of tragedies happened often in the labor camp.

One time, the labor camp guards sent my father and other laborers to an open wildland to create cultivatable fields. While the laborers were digging, they discovered a coffin covered by coal. The guards asked them to open the coffin. Once it was opened, they saw a body inside wearing an official robe of an ancient dynasty with shiny jade and gold beads attached to its clothing; it must have been buried for hundreds of years. Yet the body was preserved so well that it looked like it was buried just for a short time. Besides the body, there were many artifacts in the coffin; some of them were piled neatly outside of the coffin. My father instantly knew that the body and the funerary objects were valuable archaeological treasures. This dead person must have been an important person in history. Because the guards usually had little or no educational background, they did not know the value of the treasures. They ordered the workers to take the body and cremate it immediately without reporting to any authority. My father wanted to object but did not dare to say a word. He was helpless as he watched the guards and other workers take the body away. No one knew who took the rest of the artifacts. When he told me this story, he still questioned why the body was kept so fresh and why it was preserved so well for hundreds of years. He said, "It was as if he were sleeping. Was that because the coal kept the coffin dry or prevented oxygen from getting access to the body? Who was this official? In which dynasty did he live?" He kept these questions in his mind for many years.

During the time my father was at the labor camp in 1964, my mother was pregnant with me. Without food coupons, she struggled to find food to feed her family and worried about miscarriage due to lack of nutrition. She often went to the state-owned seafood market to pick up some fish intestines or squid mouths that were thrown away by the cleaning employees. She used those inedible parts to make a soup to drink, hoping to give me some nutrition. One day, her water broke. Mrs. Yang saw it and told her to go to the hospital immediately. I was born on that day without my father's presence; however, after I was born, my paternal grandmother came to help.

After half a year of labor-correction, public security, the Gon An, told my father that he needed to be re-educated again, and this time he would only be paid five yuan per month. There was no reason given. This news came like a bolt of lightning out of the blue. My father knew that this was not the way his life should be, so he planned his way out. First, my father pretended to accept what they had told him. He continued to work on establishing himself as a good worker and remolding his ideology. Then, after a while, he requested a short leave to see his new baby girl, who was me, and his aging mother.

When he came home, the family had a moment of happiness, but soon he could feel that the family was weighted down with anxiety. Adding a new baby did not add much joy because the city government refused to issue a resident permit for me. I could not receive a residence permit because of my parents' status: a father in the labor camp, a mother without a resident permit.

During my father's short visit at home, he held me constantly. At that time, I cried horribly at night with hunger pains because my mother lacked milk due to poor nutrition. I made so much noise at night, but my father never complained once. He just tried to comfort me and held me all throughout the night. To carry out his plan carefully, my father went back to the camp.

My mother tried to find a job, but without resident status, she couldn't work. At that time, there were no more private companies because all private economies had been eliminated. Planned economics established state monopolies. All state jobs required residency permits. Without any choice, my mother went back to her original boss, who was my father's friend, to work as a babysitter. She had to let my grandmother Nai Nai take care of my sister and me at home. I cried for food a lot; however, my grandmother could not stop me from crying, so she let me suck her dry nipples, and hopefully, I would not cry that badly; but her breasts could not pacify me.

My mother's job required her to take care of four children during the day and at night. Her salary was twelve yuan per month and two meals a day. She could only go home to see her children once a week. Sometimes when the boss had leftover rice, he would give it to my mother to bring home so that my grandmother could make fried rice for us. To save money, my mother did not use any public transportation when returning home from work. She had to walk more than two hours to get home. Although the cost of the bus fare for one trip was only 0.12 yuan, every penny was very important.

Since my paternal grandmother took care of my sister and me every day, we were not affectionate toward my mother. Once when my mother came back home, she tried to please us by handing out two candies for us, one for me and one for my sister. When she showed me the candy and said, "Ah Jade, candy! Ah Jade, come here!" I turned my back and crawled away from her. She had walked for more than two hours to save the bus fare in order to buy the candy for me, but I refused to take it. That broke her heart deeply, so even to this day, she has told me that story repeatedly. Every time she tells this story, her throat tightens, her voice still trembles.

My father came home and visited again, but this time as planned, he did not want to return to the labor camp. To avoid being taken back by the police, he could only stay for the days allowed. Before he finished the visit, my father planned everything that he must do at home. First, he sent his mother back to the countryside where she could get a food allotment in her hometown. My grandmother Nai Nai was a big help for my mother, but feeding an extra mouth on my mother's twelve yuan per month was impossible. Leaving her grandchildren was never easy. Before she left, she hugged us many times, and her eyes gazed at us, reluctant to leave. My mother held her hands and said, "Mother, don't leave. I need you. The kids need you."

"I have to go; there is no food for all of us to survive. We cannot die together."

"But once you leave, how can I go to work? Rong only makes five yuan per month in the camp."

"Don't worry, Rong will solve the problem." But Nai Nai knew that her son wouldn't be able to solve the problem.

"I am scared of living by myself with the kids. The guards may come at any time." My mother begged her to stay. The two had built a very good relationship while my father was in the labor camp, and they depended on each other for survival. Before she left, she exhorted my mother to be brave and then walked out the door. As she turned to depart, her soul seemed to attach itself to the kids. My mother ran after her and yelled, "Mother! Mother!"

My father told us a few times with great emotion about how he sent his mother back to the countryside. He said that he had never cried in his life, the only time was while he was sending his mother off on the bus. Her leaving was like his soul had been taken away from him. Tears streaming down his face as he watched his mother's image on the bus, he felt as if a knife was piercing his heart. He blamed himself because he was incapable of helping his mother, and he caused her to worry about him. He could not control his tears. There was a sudden feeling that he might not have a chance to see her again. His premonition was true, and that was the last time he ever saw her.

After my father sent his mother off, he didn't report back to the labor camp as required. Instead, he escaped. To avoid the guards catching him, he hid wherever he could. Occasionally, he came back to take a peek at his family and leave again. He stayed in his former employees' homes. If there were any signs of trouble, he would sleep in sugarcane fields, which were filled with all kinds of insects, mostly mosquitoes. He was devoured by swarms of mosquitoes. He slept in many different places to avoid capture. His was a life on the run.

CHAPTER 8

SINGLE MOTHER SURVIVING IN GUANGZHOU CITY

MY FATHER'S ABSENCE and grandmother's leaving caused my mother great difficulties living in Guangzhou around 1965. She had no job, no money, no food. Worst of all, my mother was neither a registered resident of the city nor in the countryside because she left her hometown when she was fourteen years old in 1953 before the new residency regulation was established. The village leaders thought she would not come back to her hometown again, so they removed my mother's name as a resident. A residency permit was part of the administrative order to control the migration of farmers to cities, so it would have enough laborers to work in the field and allow the government to control food distribution. In general, the permits dictated where you lived and where you could go. Everybody considered living in the cities very lucky because there were better food supplies, better education, better housing, and better health care. However, cities were unable to provide sufficient jobs and food for their residents due to the broken economy, so the government had to stop the farmers from fleeing into the cities.

As a consequence, the administration regulated that a peasant woman who married a city man must stay a peasant. As a result, my mother did not have a resident permit anywhere.

Since the Great Famine, the government had to issue coupon certificates to each citizen to buy rice, flour, sugar, meat, oil, clothing, soap, and other necessities to manage the severe shortages. Without coupons, money could not buy food and clothes. This coupon system ran nationally, but in practice, there were differences between cities and the countryside.

When I was born, only my sister, who had the only resident permit in the family, could receive the food allotment coupon from the government. In those difficult days, my mother gathered left-over vegetable leaves as the markets were closing and even picked up watermelon skins when others threw them away. Sometimes, she picked wild vegetables next to the railroad. It was hard to find anything wild in the city; whatever she picked was precious for the family. She sold some of her possessions in exchange for food. She only kept my father's materials for drawing blueprints because she thought that my father might show up at any time. Besides depending on my sister for her food allotment, my mother's side of the family spared us some food.

Although the lack of food was a big problem for our family, the worst problem was having our family considered a bad element. The guards would knock on our door at any time, day or night, to check on us and search my father. They would come in and confiscate valuable items. The first time they came, they took a Singer sewing machine, bicycles, two watches, and other things. They only left a second sewing machine, possibly because it was too heavy for them to move. My mother predicted that they were going to come again, so when her mother brought food over, she asked her to take the sewing machine away and sell it for food. She also hid the sizable gold necklace that my father had given her for their engagement. She put her gold necklace in a ceramic pot mixed with water and herbal medicine to cover it. Chinese people used to use that type of pot to boil herbal medicine. The guards overlooked this common cheap pot, and it saved my mother's gold necklace.

In those days, my mother was always afraid of knocks at the door, fearful that the guards might come back again. Her fear proved correct. The guards did come back many times, and they took more things that they thought were valuable. They took some furniture and a washbasin, but they didn't open the pot. In the end, the only things my mother had were a bed with a mosquito net, a blanket, a table, and other cheap things like my father's tools for drawing blueprints and his little flute, which my father loved to play in his leisure time, plus the herbal pot hiding the gold chain, and a big wok that my mother used to cook for my father's employees.

My mother was renting a house from a second landlord, the first having being an American who left China in 1949 to go back to the US and asked his friend's daughter to take care of the home. The owner of the house was an American doctor who went back to the US in 1949. Because the owner was a foreigner, the house was exempt from being confiscated by the government. After my father left the house, he knew that my mother could not pay the rent since she had no job, so he introduced his hometown friend Ah Wang to share the place and the rental cost. Ah Wang stayed only for a few months, then he told my mother that he would move out and leave for the city. In reality, he was planning to escape to Hong Kong. My mother later found her cousin's family to move in and share the house with us. She kept only the smallest room for the three of us. At that time, the rent was completely controlled by the government. A month's rent was twelve yuan for our family. After my mother sublet half of the house to her cousin, her rental expense was reduced to six yuan per month. Later, my mother could not afford to pay even the reduced rent, so she sublet almost the whole floor to her cousin, dropping her rent to three yuan a month, which she was able to manage by squeezing all three of us in a small room. At that time, I was a one-year-old baby and my sister was almost four years old.

When my grandmother Po Po learned about our situation, she brought us three hens from the countryside. She told my mother these hens could lay eggs every day, so the children could have some nutrition. That night, my mother dreamed her three hens laid many eggs; eggs were everywhere, eggs in the cage, in the house, in the yard, and on the porch. She dreamed her mother-in-law was making egg cakes with sugar and oil, and her children were watching with open jaws. In the middle of this dream, a knock on the door woke her up; she walked to the door and found the landlady standing in front of her to collect the rent.

The landlady reminded my mother that she had not paid rent for more than a year. My mother begged her to give her more time since she did not have money. She added, "Once my husband comes back home, then he will definitely pay you." The landlady said with an embarrassed smile: "You may pay the rent with your chickens now." My mother's sweet dream turned into a cruel reality. She took out all three hens and handed them to the landlady. At that time, these chickens could pay up to four months of rent since a hen was worth 2.50 to four yuan. Without a meat coupon, the cost of each hen was much more than that. The landlady was happy to get whatever she could.

While my father was in the labor camp and later hiding somewhere else, my mother suffered financially and psychologically. One political movement was barely over, and another movement rose ferociously like a storm. It seemed the nightmare would never end.

CHAPTER 9

THE START OF THE CULTURAL REVOLUTION

IN THE FALL OF 1966, my mother walked out of her house and saw big-character posters called "dazibao" plastered everywhere: on walls, houses, and tree trunks. Many students were holding giant portraits of Mao, beating drums, and shouting slogans as they paraded on the streets. A young, fashionably dressed woman, wearing a pair of western-style bell-bottom pants, ran desperately toward my mother. In all her stylish clothes, you could tell that she was from Hong Kong. About a hundred feet away from her was a young man who had a piece of a red armband with the words RED GUARD on his sleeve. He was holding a pair of scissors and chasing after her. The woman looked at my mother and cried out in despair, "Mrs! Mrs! Help!" Suddenly, she tripped over some rough surface and fell. She had been hoping that she could get into someone's house and escape from the Red Guard. My mother rushed to her, but the Red Guard pushed his way between them. He said, "What a pair of evil pants! Western bourgeoisie! A capitalist would never escape our eyes." Then he cut her pants from bottom to top. The woman cried out and started shivering uncontrollably—she thought the Red Guard wanted to kill her.

The "Great Proletarian Cultural Revolution" (see Appendix A-7) started furiously. It was supposed to change the old culture and old establishment in China. The actual reason behind this was that Mao Zedong, the Chairman of the communist party (not the president of China), felt that his power had been limited by his own government system, and his policies of the Great Leap Forward and People's Commune had been criticized. He wrote the first dazibao to start the Cultural Revolution. He accused the government officials of going in a capitalist direction and leading the country to go back to the old regime. He was calling young people to rise up and demolish the establishment, the government system. As a result, many people, especially students, followed the call and formed Red Guards and anti-authority rebel organizations. The country was in complete chaos, with riots everywhere. All the means of transportation were free for the Red Guards to ride on to spread the "revolution" to the whole country; schools were closed; factories stopped production. In the capital of China, Beijing, Chairman Mao greeted the Red Guards from Tiananmen Gate, gave them his blessing, and mobilized his followers. The Cultural Revolution provoked hatred between people by creating many "enemies" with nine categories: landlords, rich peasants, counter-revolutionaries, bad elements, rightists, traitors, foreign agents, capitalists, and intellectuals (including teachers). The Cultural Revolution also had the goal of destroying the "Four Olds": old culture, old customs, old habits, and old ways of thinking.

During that time, the streets were flooded with young Red Guards with red armbands and red flags. They shouted with loudspeakers: "Our great leader, great teacher, great commander, and great helmsman, Chairman Mao said to carry the Cultural Revolution to the very end!" or "Highest order: Chairman Mao's saying is the truth, one sentence is equivalent to ten thousand sentences!" Another loudspeaker would follow: "Our Great Chairman Mao teaches us: A revolution is not a dinner party or writing an essay or painting a picture or doing embroidery; it cannot be so refined, so leisurely, and gentle . . . A revolution is an insurrection, an act of violence by which one class over-throws another." They stormed the government build-ings shouting, "Down with capitalist router XXX!" They called the government officials by name and beat them with great violence. They destroyed temples, palaces, and tombs, and burned priceless books, paintings, sculptures, and antiques. The cities were crowded with these rioters and resounded with the loud sounds of drums and gongs.

Eventually, these events escalated, and the rioters be-came more violent and armed. They invaded houses and offices; humiliated, terrorized, and often killed their vic-tims. The Red Guards also argued with each other since they formed different organizations and fought for pow-er between those groups. All of them claimed that they were the true revolutionaries and accused others of being counter-revolutionaries.

At that time, my Gong Gong (grandfather) had stom-ach pain, and he went to a local hospital. The doctors told him that he might need surgery, but they did not have ad-vanced equipment to check on him, so they referred him to a city hospital in Guangzhou. Gong Gong brought food and personal belongings to Guangzhou, and he prepared to stay there for a thorough checkup. The doctors checked on him and suggested to him that he needed surgery as soon as possible. On the day of surgery, all the residents in the city warned each other not to go out because the Red Guards were fighting each other. There were already many dead bodies hanging on the trees in one street in Guangzhou City. Blood was everywhere. All the facto-ries and stores were closed. The young Red Guards took over the hospital, and some of them treated patients who had emergencies; doctors performed surgeries under the eyes of the Red Guards. There were numerous accidents because the Red Guards had no medical knowledge; the doctors were anxious and fearful. Gong Gong was nervous about staying in the city for a week because violent fights and killings occurred every day. As a result, he went back to his home without proper treatment.

Once he got home, the first thing people told him that there were many dead bodies floating in the Pearl River. Some of the bodies were tied together; my aunt and uncle even saw a woman with a baby floating together. The bodies swelled up badly, almost popping out of their clothing. Some of the bodies flowed alone to the canal. The village leader sent a few brave men to push the bodies back to the river. My grandfather felt lucky that he was able to get back home. He stayed at home for about two years, and he treated his stomach problem with herbs. For these two years, he took care of me despite his health issue.

My family was targeted by the Red Guards, and my father was in hiding. Every time my Big Aunt Guishen's husband Zhongbao, the former judge in Guangzhou City, heard somebody died at the crossroad traffic control pavilion where the Red Guard liked to hang or beat the so-called "enemies," he sent his daughter to check out to see if the body was my father's. After they confirmed the body was not my father's, they were relieved but still worried. My cousin, who was about ten years older than I, was horrified to check on those dead bodies. At the time, my mother did not know where my father was, nor did she know her relatives were so concerned about my father's situation because they did not want to tell her how dangerous the situation was.

Around 1967, as a result of all these Red Guard and

Revolutionary anti-authority rebel organizations' movements, the Chinese government was completely paralyzed, and Chairman Mao assumed his absolute power. Later, to stop the violence and killings, Chairman Mao sent the military troops loyal to him to take over the government and even crack down on some of the rebel organizations that supported his agenda. However, the economy collapsed, there were no jobs and no food to support hundreds of millions of young people, and Red Guards flooded the cities. Therefore, Mao called another movement to send these cities' students and residents to the countryside (see Appendix A-9) as the "bigger university" to be re-educated by the working class. Thousands of young people paraded on the street, and loudspeakers announced: "Chairman Mao's newest order! It is necessary for educated youths go to the countryside to receive re-education from the poor and middle-class peasants…" So there was another wave of millions of people traveling.

The chaos of the Cultural Revolution provided opportunities for my father to escape from the labor camp. Since so many young people and Red Guards traveled all over the country to carry out the Cultural Revolution, people who were in trouble like my father could blend in with the traveling crowd. However, there were still risks since these people were not young and could get caught and be identified. My father traveled to several places to see if he could hide and make a living. He first went to Dongguan, seventy kilometers away from Guangzhou City. It was not hard to make a living there. His younger brother, Ning Chen, also went there with him. He was much younger than my father and had never joined any organization before, so he was not a target of the Red Guards. Ning was still a kid, so he made friends with the son of a local leader.

One day, this friend told Ning that his father would seize all the migrants. Ning gave thirty yuan to his friend and begged him not to capture my father and him. The young man said okay, that he would tell his dad. When my father found out that the leader wanted to capture them, he immediately told the other outsiders and made his escape. His brother was naive and told my father that the son of the leader promised not to catch them, so they could continue to stay in Dongguan, but my father dragged him to leave with the other outsiders.

My father felt that Dongguan was too close to Guangzhou City, so he went to Shaoguan, two-hundred-forty kilometers away from Guangzhou City. It is a beautiful scenic mountainous area near the northern part of Guangdong province on the border of the Hunan and Jiangxi provinces. The place was close to an autonomous county. When he found that he could make a living there without running into somebody who could recognize him, he sent his friend to pick up my mother to join him. They would be reunited at last.

CHAPTER 10

A VAGRANT LIFE

WHILE MY MOTHER WAS STRUGGLING in this hard period in Guangzhou City in the winter of 1966, one day,
a mysterious man came to our house who claimed to be
my father's labor camp friend. He told my mother that
my father was waiting for her. He asked my mother to
prepare to leave the city and told her he would come back
to bring her to my father. My mother looked at my sister
and me. She felt uneasy about making the decision to
move because I was just a toddler; she could not take me
on a long trip to places she did not even know. My father
was a fugitive, so it would be very difficult to escape with
me if we were chased by guards. Still, she took important documents like our birth certificates and my father's
college diploma, the flute, and some of my father's tools
for drawing blueprints. She decided to leave me with my
grandmother, so she brought me to her mother's countryside house with those small possessions. Then she and my
sister left with my father's friend to join him. From that
day on, my maternal grandparents took care of me. Ever
since I was born, my only impression of my father was of
his tools for drawing blueprints and the little flute.

My mother did not tell anybody in the neighborhood
that she was leaving except the landlord. She took my
older sister to the train with my father's friend and de-
parted from the city. Their train was headed to Shaoguan
where my father was. Some of the people there were of
the Hakkas tribe. They were people of Northern China

who escaped from the wars in the Song Dynasty about one thousand years. They settled down in Guangdong and spoke a different dialect. Some were Yao tribe who lived in an autonomous county. The government did not pay much attention to this mountainous area occupied by some minorities. My mother had never seen so many mountains.

Once my mother reunited with my father, they were very excited and told each other what they had been through while they were separated. My father was not alone; there was a big group of vagrants who were former landlords, business owners, and intellectuals such as professors, engineers, and philosophers, even a composer. There were also so-called "right-wing" communist cadres who had been removed from power and targeted by the left-wing cadres. They all had left their homes to become vagrants. Some of them were single, but many of them fled with their families; some of them even brought three generations. There my father met his childhood best friend, Wu Lin, who was from a very rich family before communists took over China. His family used to own a large quantity of land. The family had servants and maids and hired private teachers at home for their children. Therefore, Lin had never attended school outside, but his knowledge was very broad; he was good in literature as well as mathematics. Although he never entered school in his life, he wrote many touching poems. During the land reform time, his mother strangled herself. Many of his family members died; only his older brother was able to escape to Hong Kong.

My mother and my older sister joined a large group of vagrants. They endured the hardships of an arduous journey. Most of the time, they had to eat in the open, sleep on the grass, and bathe in the rivers and streams. When they saw mountains in front of them, they trudged over them. When rivers blocked their way, my father would watch my sister and their possessions and let my mother swim across to the other side first. Then my father held my sister to cross the river. Once he reached the other side of the river, he left my sister to my mother, and then he swam back to get their possessions. They could have paid 0.05 yuan for a ferry, but they wanted to save the money for food. They did not have a stable residence and traveled from one village to another, but they used their talents to earn money and food. They carried only a few necessities, like a mosquito net and a comforter for sleeping, toothbrushes, and pots for making meals.

One time they passed by a beautiful place where water and mountains added radiance and beauty to each other. My father enjoyed a moment in the wild scenery and went swimming in the water. My mother held my sister to take a bath. When my sister took her little legs out of the water, three leeches were sucking her legs. My mother was terrified and tried to pull them off, but the leeches sucked onto the skin very hard. They seemed to have the ability to numb their victim. My mother was alone, scared, and devastated. She desperately called my father to help, but my father had swum already far away. She could only see my father's head like a black dot flowing on the water. She was helpless, with tears streaming down her cheeks, which triggered my sister to cry. A passerby said that my sister may still bleed after pulling out the leeches. He suggested my mother use fire to burn them. My mother found a match from their possessions. She lighted a small stick and held it with wide eyes and a pounding pulse. At the same time, she warned my sister not to move and started to burn them. The leeches dropped one by one. Watching the creepy, slimy, bloody leeches wiggle out, she almost threw up. Even though the leeches gave my mother a scare, the most horrifying time was while they were walking, a snake suddenly came out and crossed over my sister's foot. My mother freaked out and froze, but she held her breath and did not alert my sister. She worried that my sister's reaction would disturb the snake, and it would bite her. From that day on, my mother feared being in the wilderness.

Since my father was a contractor, he gathered a couple of people to help the communes and villagers to build houses, offices, and stone arch bridges. The local leaders would pay for their labor or offer food. Sometimes my father got some small jobs like helping people build chimneys, and once they helped one family build a chimney, then the whole village would ask them to build chimneys. So my parents did not have to worry about a job for a while. In the meantime, they had to watch out for any signs of disturbance from local cadres or militias.

In those days, my parents usually stayed in huts, cowsheds, or abandoned houses where somebody was hanged. Nobody dared to live in those houses because the local people believed that ghosts lived there. One time they even built a tent next to a new grave. The fresh flowers and paper money remained on top of the grave. Sometimes they lived in old temples, those temples were once very popular for worship, but during the Cultural Revolution, people were not allowed to practice any religion. Worshiping was considered one of the Four Olds. Anybody who still worshiped gods was punished.

They once stayed in an ancestral temple used to worship ancestors of the village before the communist regime.

There were many ancestral tablets, and each had the name of a family's grandparents to great grandparents. There were a few coffins that were put next to the wall. Those coffins were prepared by the families of the elders in the village. No one dared to go there at night. One day my sister saw some people taking a coffin out, and the next day some people were holding the same coffin as they walked out of the village. There was a line of people who were crying behind the box. She was scared and learned that the box had a dead body in it. She did not have the nerve to go back to the temple again. My parents had no place to sleep since their daughter refused to go back there. So they built a tent far away from the temple and close to the water. My mother thought that she could get the water easily, but a local woman stopped by and warned my mother that the water had blood flukes, a type of parasitic worm that can be fatal if you get it into your body.

Once, my father got a project from a local leader to build a hydraulic system that could bring water up to the terraced fields on the mountain. The leader had this idea for a long time but could not find anyone who could design and build it. He knew the vagrants had many talents, so he asked my father if he could build a hydraulic system for his people. My father said yes instantly without asking what would be involved. Then the local leader ordered my father to dismantle an old temple that was at least a few hundred years old. My father asked, "Why you want me to dismantle an old temple before I build the hydraulic system?" My father thought it was not necessary to demolish the temple. The leader seemed to understand my father's feelings but stated, "The water source was next to that temple." My father did not want to destroy any old temple because it was an important historical site. He suggested that he could find another water source somewhere other than the temple site or just build the hydraulic system without damaging the temple. The leader explained that his superior ordered them to demolish the temple because it was considered to be a Four Olds and his own village people refused to destroy it. That was why he wanted to use outside people to do the job. My father did not have any choice; he did not want to be accused of not following the Cultural Revolution's political order to "Destroy the Four Olds." Before he dismantled it, he prayed, "God, if you really exist in here, please don't blame me; it is the leader who forced me to do it."

Later, my father, with other vagrants, got another project to build a theater. A handsome man by the name of Song was an architect in the vagrant group. He drew a blueprint of the theater, including the lighting, sound system, wiring, and audience capacity—everything that a theater needed. My father and the other vagrants became Song's assistants. All the vagrants had nicknames; none of them used their real names so that the local officials could not track them. For example, people called my father "Big Mark" because of a big birthmark on his chin. My father's childhood friend Wu Lin changed his last name from Lin to Chan. They were very excited that they could do something meaningful. Within days the theater was shaping up. While everybody was happy, a burst of sweet melody floated to everyone's ears, and the composer was happily playing his two-stringed musical instrument called an "erhu." When he finished a piece of music, my mother walked to him and said,

"How could you be in the mood to bring an erhu with you considering our situation?"

"Well, this erhu is my family treasure. My father asked

me to protect it before he died," he replied.

When the job was almost done, except for the roof and wiring, some cadres came from the commune. They were searching for the "bad elements" in the vagrant group. The leader who ordered vagrants to build the theater was very anxious because if those vagrants were caught by the cadres, who would do the roof, the wiring, and other unfinished jobs? With great risk to himself, he told the cadres that the people who built the theater were all good citizens, and he affirmed that they were not going to do anything harmful to the country.

A cadre said, "How can I trust you?"

"I signed your documents to vouch for their loyalty to the government. Anything happens, then come to me."

"What do you think who you are? You are only a lower rank leader. We need somebody who has a higher rank than you to sign the paper."

"I am going to get my superior."

A short, broad-shouldered, older man came in. A big portion of his left shoulder and arm had very thick calluses. These thick skin marks showed that he had carried a rifle for a long time. He had been in the People's Liberation Army for most of his life. The vagrants called him "Dabusi," meaning "immortal" because he fought a long-time war and survived. After the civil war, he and the deputy leader settled down in Guangdong and became local leaders. The two signed their names on the paper to guarantee all the vagrants were good citizens. After the cadres left, they exhorted the vagrants, again and again, asking them not to leave. So everyone stayed and finished the job, except for one couple with a boy who ran when the cadres left. Within days, the authorities caught them. No one knew that family's fate.

The deputy leader and Dabusi were knowledgeable and less radical than other officials. They knew what type of people these vagrants were. The two usually showed off in front of the vagrants and bragged about how they had fought with the Kuomintang Chiang Kai-shek's army during the civil war. They said that the Kuomintang soldiers died everywhere in the town nearby, bodies piled up on one another, blood flowed on the ground. The vagrants listened to their stories with curiosity. Dabusi showed his arm to the vagrants and said, "I am from the north with the communist army, but I didn't walk here. I crawled to the south. This portion of thick skin was the place I held my rifle while crawling." He pushed up his sleeves to show it off. He added, "We fought from north to south and hardly stood up while fighting. Bullets had no eyes; they were flying everywhere. Anyone that stood up might easily lose their life." He stood up and went back to his office. After Dabusi left, the deputy leader let out a sigh and said, "So many people died." The composer picked up his erhu and played a piece of music; the sad melody vibrated off the mountain and ocean, his music touching all the vagrants' souls.

The vagrants could not stay in one place for a long time because they worried that the authorities might catch them again. Sometimes they finished one job, then left that place and walked for hours until they found another job. My sister was young, only about five years old. She walked with my parents and the other vagrants for more than ten hours a day. Her feet had blisters, blood bled out from her little toes, but she never cried. She walked and walked, following the adults quietly. One time she was too tired and fell to the ground on her stomach. My mother called her gently, "Ah Sue, are you okay?" but she didn't reply. My mother picked her up and called out loudly, "Ah Sue! Ah Sue! My little treasure, please don't scare me. Wake up!" Again, still no reply. My father put down his luggage, took my sister from my mother's hands, and shook her. She opened her eyes. My sister was so tired she had fallen into a deep sleep while she was walking. Every time my mother mentioned this, I could see her heart was broken.

There were two other girls who were the same age as my sister. One of the girls traveled with her parents and grandfather. Her mother was a teacher, and her father was a high school principal. He had a fake name called "Wang Laoji"; it was the brand name of a famous Chinese herbal tea. Her grandfather was a professor at a university in Guangdong. He used to live in the US before 1949 and answered the call of the new Chinese government to return to China to serve his motherland. However, his patriotic act resulted in him being charged as a "foreign spy" in the Cultural Revolution. Because he was considered a "class enemy," so, too, were his son, daughter-in-law, and his grandchild, and they all had to suffer with him. They did not know anything about construction work, but they loved to work for my father. No matter where my father went, the whole family followed him. They knew that my father would be able to find a job so they would not starve. My father would teach them, and they were always willing to learn. One day their small girl fell from a bridge and fractured her skull. Her mother held her and desperately asked God to help. My mother saw the little girl's brain, like tofu inside, and a very small piece of bone hanging off the head. The girl's father put the bone back in place and wrapped her head skillfully with a piece of fabric that was torn from a clean cloth. He seemed to have some medical knowledge, so no wonder he had the name of Wang Lao-ji. He could not bring the girl to the doctor. If they went to the hospital, the government would catch them. Her grandfather's health was so poor that he could not help at all. Unbelievably, the girl was able to walk again the next day. A few days later, the family left without telling anyone. Some of the vagrants thought they brought the girl back to the city to find medical care. Later, my parents found out that the couple got arrested soon after they left. Years passed and my parents still worried about that family, wondering if they were alive.

The other girl who played with my sister was given away to the village people by her parents. The parents planned to escape to Hong Kong, so they thought that they were not capable of bringing her while they were roaming around the dangerous terrain. Anyone attempting to escape to Hong Kong was considered a traitor. To this day, when my sister mentions her two little friends during her time of wandering, she always wonders how those girls are doing right now. Are they still alive?

There was an eighteen-year-old young man who traveled along with other vagrants. He was a humble man and always willing to learn. No one knew his background, but for sure, he must have been a son of a landlord or a "bad element." One time this young man did not come out from his cow shed. My mother went in to check on him and found he was lying on his bed. He had very bad diarrhea, or dysentery, so there was blood and mucus in his stool. He seemed to be dying, but there was no hospital or doctor around. My mother picked up some wild weeds and boiled them with water for him. After he drank it, he recovered. That knowledge of herbal medicine was passed down from generation to generation in the Chinese countryside. In those bitter days, they all tried to help each other. My mother still plants these herbs and tells people about their functions.

One time, the group went to another village. The village leader asked my father and his crew to build an office for them. When my father and his crew finished the job, they went to the leader and expected to get their pay. The head of the village asked my father where his crew came from. He said that he had to get a certified official letter to prove that they came from a legitimate organization in order to pay them. To survive, my father could not tell him the truth, so he told him that they were from a construction unit in Guangzhou City and that he would go back to his place to provide a certificate letter for him. The whole crew relied on this payment to buy food and to survive. My father had no choice but made up a fictitious construction organization. He went back to his place and used a sweet potato to make a stamp with the name of "Guangzhou City Second Construction Team." He wrote a fake certification letter and stamped it. He took that letter to the village head and got the payment they deserved. He distributed the money to his crew and told them to run as soon as possible.

They walked to many towns and counties in south China, including Shaoguan city, Lechang town, Yinhua town, Longgui town, Yiliu town, Lishi town, Huaping town, Renhua County, Danxia Mountain, Daqiao town, and Volcano town. One day, my mother felt nauseated, and she was too tired to walk around. From her experience of her previous pregnancy, she knew that she might be pregnant again. When she told my father, he had a moment of happiness, but he knew that they could not raise one more child while they were roaming from one mountain to the next and running from one village to another. After considering carefully, they reluctantly decided to abort the fetus; they knew that their child would not have a residence permit and his or her survival was completely dependent on it.

My father said, "You need to go back to the city to get the abortion. It is not safe to do any procedure in this desolate area. Besides, no one will arrest you when you go back."

"How about you?"

"Don't worry about me. I can take care of myself. By the way, take our daughter with you. It is not good for a child to wander around with us." My father counted all their savings. They had about fifteen yuan and three pounds of food coupons. He told my mother to take all of them. My mother insisted that she give one five-yuan bill and a three pound coupon back to my father and told him not to use them unless it was absolutely necessary. My father said, "You need money to see the doctor. After the surgery, go back to your mother and get a good rest."

My mother brought my sister back to the city. She ended her vagrant life of about three years with my father. Years later, my mother regretted that she didn't stay with my father. She said, "No matter how hard your life is, as long as your husband is with you, you don't have to be alone in the difficult times." After my mother left, my father went with some of his friends, including Wu Lin, to Huiyang, which is closer to Hong Kong. My father decided to escape the country. Leaving China was the only way to survive.

CHAPTER 11

REJOINING MY MOTHER AND FIGHTING FOR A RESIDENCE PERMIT

MY MOTHER QUIT THE VAGRANT LIFE and left the group of fugitives that included my father in the winter of 1968. She returned to Guangzhou City with my seven-year-old sister. She had no place to stay, so she stayed in my father's younger cousin Guijing's place (whom I called "Little Aunt") for a few days. Then, she went back to her home village in the countryside of Zhongshan to pick me up. At that time, I lived with my maternal grandmother, grandfather, aunt, and hard of hearing uncle.

I still remember the first time I met my mother and my sister in the countryside. It was at night before I went to sleep. A small kerosene lamplight was faint, and it shone rather unsteadily, casting a weak glow over the living room. Po Po took off my old jacket and attempted to repair it under the dim light.

"This is un-patchable. The fabric is too old." She talked to herself and put the jacket on the table. There were so many holes, big and small, and old dark pieces of cotton rolled out of the fabric. My grandmother tried to put the cotton back in place.

My tenth aunt, who was my mother's youngest sister, walked in and said, "This jacket is older than I am. It used to belong to my old sister." She brought a pot of hot water and poured it into a washbasin. She tested the temperature of the water first, then put my feet into the washbasin.

While she was washing my feet, someone knocked on the door and opened it. Cold air blew into the house, and the rush of air almost blew out the light. A beautiful woman with naturally curly hair came in with a girl next to her. They looked very different than the locals. The girl had two braids. They stood at the door entrance for a moment and stared at me. The woman called "Mom" to my grandmother then, "Ah Jade!" toward me.

"You are back! Come in, don't stand in front of the door." Po Po said.

"Ah Jade! Call her Mommy," my aunt said gently. I did not know the woman was my "mommy."

"Ah Jade, be a good girl, call her Mommy, hurry!" My aunt extorted me again. I hurriedly clung to my aunt.

"Ah Jade, come to Mommy." My mother extended her arms to me. I refused her hug but was more interested in the girl she brought over. The girl watched me with kindness.

She walked toward me, "Little sister, this is our mommy." I looked at both and examined them with curiosity.

"She is quiet. Now she is still barely able to walk. She could only walk for a very short distance at a time." My grandmother added, "We have to carry her all around. Her bones are soft and cannot hold her body weight."

My aunt coaxed me and let my mother hug me. My mother held her breath in an attempt to hide any sound that wanted to escape from her mouth. She felt guilty that she did not take good care of her daughter.

This was the night my mother came back after dropping me with my grandparents two years before when I was little more than a year old.

My grandfather was very sick at that time. In one of his final days, my mother went to see him at his bedside. He pointed to his stomach and said, "I have a big lump in here in my stomach. Can you feel it?"

"Yes, it is a lump, and it is very hard."

"I have so much pain. I know I am not going to live long. I cannot help you anymore."

"Don't worry. I will be fine."

"How is Rong doing? Does he have a job right now?"

My mother almost cried in front of him but held back her tears. She could not tell him that her husband was still in the labor camp or hiding somewhere unknown.

"Yes, he is working."

"I am worried about your daughter. She is four years old already and still doesn't know how to walk. Hopefully, she is not handicapped. I will protect her after I die."

I was behind my mother, but I didn't fully understand their conversation. I didn't even know Rong was my father, but I could feel my mother was sad because she was in tears. A few days later, my grandfather passed away. He probably died of colon cancer.

After the reunion, my mother was trying to find a place to live. My grandmother told her, "Life is difficult already. You need to get the residence permits for you and her. They are the root of your lives."

My mother first tried to stay in Guangzhou City by applying for a residence permit for each of us, because in the city the coupons were issued monthly or quarterly to registered city residents. The benefits were much better than those in the countryside. For example, in our countryside, each member of the production team could only get two feet and six inches of fabric per year. Each person in the city was able to get coupons for anywhere between twenty-eight to thirty-five pounds of food per month and twelve feet of fabric per year, as well as coupons to buy daily necessities like cooking oil, cigarettes, soap, and more. The medical services were much better than in the countryside. Therefore, in the eyes of the country dwellers, living in the city was like living in heaven.

During the Cultural Revolution from 1966 to 1976, the country was in turmoil, the peasants did not spend much time working in the fields, and the factory workers in the city did not produce goods. As a result, there was a great shortage of food and all sorts of everyday necessities. Even if you had money and coupons, the government-owned stores might not have anything on the shelves, so once some goods showed up in the stores, people formed long lines outside. That was what I used to see and experience when I was a young child. However, there were some fancy food items—like big dried scallops, dry salt squid, dry abalone, and smoked whole ham legs that Chinese people considered delicacies—displayed on the front of the store shelves. There was no price tag on them because it was not for sale to the local people. I was curious and asked a cashier how much the dry squid was for per pound. He said, "It is for foreigners, you cannot buy it." I told him that I just wanted to know. He replied, "Go away." It was for showing to the foreigners or Hong Kong people who visited China to give them the image that Chinese people ate well.

Yet for my mother, without money and coupons, buying food was much harder than it was for ordinary citizens. Therefore, survival in the city was almost impossible for her. Also, she was deemed among the most unwelcome people in the country as the wife of a "Five Black Categories" (landlords, rich peasants, counter-revolutionaries, bad elements, and rightists), who were public enemies. Because of that, she had even been thrown out twice by close relatives. One time, after trying to apply for the resident permit, my mother returned to her old rental house. She had sublet it to her cousin before she left the city. The house was quite big, and her table, bed, and a few household goods, including a big wok, were still in there. My mother carried me on her back and held my sister with one hand.

Her cousin opened the door. He looked at my mother coldly and said, "What are you doing here?"

"We just came back to the city and had nowhere to go. Please let us stay for just one night," my mother begged him.

"No, you cannot stay here."

My sister recognized the house. She was so tired of walking all day, so she immediately sprawled onto a chair and fell asleep. When he saw my sister asleep on the chair, he yelled: "You need to get out now!" Then he called neighborhood security to throw us out on the street. My mother was speechless. Tears were streaming down her face; the salty water flowing into her mouth so that she tasted her sorrow, but he could not feel it. I was crying on her back, and my sister was scared and held my mother's hand tightly. We walked and walked on random streets. It was the darkest night.

We had no money, no transportation, nowhere to go. Finally, my mother remembered one of my father's former employees, Mr. Liangjiang Wu, who was a kind person. Perhaps there we could find help? She carried me and held my sister. We walked another two hours to arrive at his house around midnight. She knocked on the door. Mr. Wu and his wife were already asleep. They woke up and opened the door surprised to see us. Before my mother could say anything, they immediately realized that we were in trouble and asked us to come into their home. His wife took me down from my mother's back and put me on the bed.

Despite my mother's best efforts, we didn't get the resident permits for my mother and me. Without it, we could not get coupons to buy food. At that time, only my sister had a residence permit. It was not possible to survive in the city for the three of us with only one child's food coupon. Therefore, my mother tried again and again with numerous trips to Guangzhou City. Each time, she brought us to the city government building.

One afternoon after another failure to acquire the resident permit, my mother walked out of the government building with my sister and me. It was windy and thundering. My mother knew that soon there would be a downpour, but she had no umbrella or raincoat. She stood in front of the building, watching people hurrying back and forth. She suddenly decided to go to her original house. My mother carried me on her back and held my sister's hand as we ran to the house. She asked her cousin to give her old wok back, the wok my mother used to cook for my father's employees. It was a downpour with thunderstorms. Her cousin dumped the wok out; my mother took over the wok. She put it on top of my head and used an old baby comforter to wrap me on her back. On top of me, the old big black iron wok covered me like an umbrella to keep me from getting wet, but my two legs still got soaked because the wok could not cover my whole body. After that, we went to my father's older cousin Guishen's house, whom we called Big Aunt. She was also labeled as a "Five Black Category" since her husband had a history of working for the old government. When she opened her door and saw us, she was afraid to let us into her house because it might cause her some political trouble. At that time, anybody who accepted us could be considered to be hiding counter-revolutionaries.

She said, "You can't stay here."

"Can we stay until the rain stops?" my mother asked.

"Go away! Go away!" Big Aunt insisted. She shut the door.

Once again, we were standing on the street in the torrential rain. The whole city was covered in darkness. The streets were empty because people went to shelters. Only the three of us were soaked on the street with nowhere to go.

We only had one more relative living in Guangzhou City who was the "Little Aunt Guijing," but her home was on the other side of the Pearl River. My mother took all her money out, just enough to buy tickets to take the ferry to reach Little Aunt's house. Little Aunt was very nice to us. She immediately brought out her daughter's clothes and helped my sister and me to change our wet clothes. Then, she asked us, "Are you hungry?" We nodded. She sent out her husband to buy a chicken so she could cook a warm meal. My sister and I each got a chicken leg, and since we hadn't eaten meat for a long time, we devoured the chicken legs with a wild hunger, gobbling them up within minutes. The three of us stayed in her house that night. To this day, I still remember how delicious that chicken was, and for years I thought they ate meat every day. Years later, we went to Little Aunt's home during dinner time, and I saw only one simple vegetable dish on the dining table for the whole family. I realized how generous and kind she had been. That warm meal with chicken was a special treat for us, not because we were important people, but the opposite, because we were poor and in trouble.

Chapter 12

THE RED SHOES

SINCE WE NO LONGER HAD A HOME in the city, the three of us went to my grandmother's house in the countryside. Despite the hardship, my mother did not give up. She fought for residence permits every day. She had to. Without them, we would become homeless.

Her persistence bore a cost. After one visit, the city officials not only rejected her request, they also revoked my sister's resident permit in the city. They claimed that it was their mistake to issue the city residence permit for my sister when she was born. That meant our whole family wouldn't have food coupons or permission to work or go to school. We couldn't survive in the city. Therefore, my mother went to the highest provincial authority in the state to petition for residence permits.

At that time, my mother not only suffered physical exhaustion, but each trip to the state agency broke her down psychologically. Time after time, she took my sister and me by boat from our hometown in Zhongshan to Guangzhou City. We usually boarded an old ferryboat the night before from a local port in Xiaolan, the nearest town, thirteen kilometers from our village. The boat traveled slowly on the Pearl River on its overnight trip. We slept at the lowest level, where there were no windows. It was like a huge box with many people sitting or lying on the floor. Each person was assigned to a small space defined by small wooden strips. My mother, sister, and I squeezed into one space normally assigned to one person because my mother did not have enough money to buy a space for each of us. Falling asleep was hard because it was too crowded and noisy—the adults were chatting, the babies crying. Sometimes I got bored and walked to the upper level of the boat to look at the river and smell the fresh air. I had never thought the water was dangerous, but my mother called me back and warned me not to go on deck by myself. By dawn, the boat arrived in Guangzhou City. We had traveled there many times, and each time my mother went to a government office building where two armed guards stood at the front gate. I did not know why she had to go there, but I feared the sharp pointy knife on top of the soldiers' rifles that glistened in the sun. My sister and I waited outside the gate while my mother went into the building for long hours.

One of these trips I remember the most was a chilly winter day in 1969. The wind blew through Guangzhou city, stinging my skin. After waiting for a long time outside of the government building, my mother finally came out with a sad face. On the trip back, holding my mother's hand as my older sister held the other, we walked along the Pearl River. The bleak gray clouds were reflected in the dark river water flowing next to us. My feet were hurting and frozen. Both my sister and I were still wearing old summer plastic shoes. At five years old and unable to keep up with my mother, I was dragged along, sobbing and muttering, "My feet hurt, my feet hurt." My shoes had first belonged to my older cousin. After a few years, they became my sister's shoes. When they would no longer fit on her feet, they became mine. By that time, the shoes were barely wearable. The tops were cracked open and then repaired by my mother, who burned scrap plastic pieces onto them from other broken shoes.

We passed a state-owned store that displayed a pair of red-colored children's shoes among the things in the window. I was excited to see the red shoes and muttered, "I want shoes. I want shoes!" My sister whispered in my ear, "Ask Mom to buy the shoes." So I begged my mother, "Mama, buy the red shoes!" Our mother looked at our little, red, swelling feet with a sad and hopeless face. She said nothing, just held our hands, and walked away toward the Pearl River. This time we walked along the river edge where we could see the strong river current flowing. Normally my mother did not allow us to stand too close to the riverbank because it was so dangerous. This time, holding our hands, she led us closer and closer to the edge of the river, then stopped at the edge, staring emotionlessly at the rapidly flowing water. My mother tightly squeezed our hands for a while then released them, gazing at us with a strange look. Afraid that something was wrong, I cried loudly, which triggered my sister to cry.

While we were crying and wiping our tears, my mother unexpectedly disappeared. At first, we thought she had just stepped away from us, but after a while, when she didn't come back, we became worried and kept calling, "Mama! Mama!" We walked back and forth along the Pearl River's edge but could not find her. We felt something was very wrong, and my body began to shake; I started to cry loudly. Many people were walking and biking on the street, and some of them stopped, looked at us, and seemingly had questions to ask but walked away. We walked back to the place where mother had left us, hoping she would show up. A tall, middle-aged woman saw us and said, "Poor children, their parents don't want them anymore." She shook her head, let out a sigh, and turned in another direction. As she walked away, my sister started to cry with me. She feared being left with no one to take care of us.

I asked, "Where is Mama? Where is Mama?"

"She will be back," my sister said, though she sounded scared and was still crying. The feeling of insecurity built up in my body when I saw my sister crying. We saw some buses and bicycles on a big bridge nearby, so we ran to the bridge. From a distance, we saw a skinny woman standing, leaning out over the guardrail, facing the water with her hair blowing in the wind. My sister and I ran as fast as we could to her, calling, "Mama! Mama!" She remained where she was, and I took her hand and said, "Mom, let's go home. I was wrong. I don't want shoes anymore." She hugged both of us, tears falling. Holding our hands again, she walked away from the bridge. She knew that it was her responsibility to raise us because our father was still running for his life from one place to another.

In my young mind, I thought my mother walking away was my fault because I had asked for shoes. Later, I began to understand what may have happened on that chilly day. I realized that my mother intended to commit suicide at the Pearl River, and our lives could all have ended. After that, my sister and I never asked our mother to buy anything for us. Whatever she gave us, we wore it. I got used to having bare feet when I was a child. One time, she used small leftover pieces of cloth to make a pair of beautiful shoes for me. The fabric was red with flowers, and it was absolutely alluring. I was so happy and excited about the shoes that I wore them to bed.

My mother fought for residence permits for many years. After we came back from another unsuccessful trip to the government office in Guangzhou City, my mother sat on the bed and stared at a small kerosene lamp, which was the only light in our house. She talked to herself in a whimper. Later, she blew out the light and went to bed with a mosquito net surrounding her. She was still mumbling, her voice at one moment sad and at another angry. I was in the outside room and was afraid to walk in. Had I done something wrong and gotten in trouble again? My muscles tensed. After she was in bed, I tiptoed to my bed and started to lie down.

My sister pulled me and spoke quietly in my ear. "Tonight, we cannot sleep. We must take turns watching Mommy. She may be going to kill herself. I have been watching her for a while already. Now you are going to watch her until you get very tired, then wake me up."

As a six-year-old child, I had no idea what was going on. I was scared. I sat inside the mosquito net. I tried to sit up straight so I did not fall asleep. The moonlight shone through the small window. In the dim moonlight, I heard my mother still mumbling. I did not understand what her words meant. The sounds of her sobbing stopped. My eyes were too tired, so I woke my sister up. She sat up fast and immediately asked me how my mother was doing. I whispered to her that our mother had just gone to sleep. My sister said, "Now, you go to sleep. I am going to watch her." A rooster called in the early morning when the sky was still dark. I opened my eyes and saw my sister was sleeping next to me. I jerked upright in my bed and immediately tiptoed to my mother's bed to check on her. She was safe and sleeping. I was relieved.

My mother was lucky that her suicide attempt was not successful. During the Cultural Revolution, thousands of the intelligentsia, landlords, rightists, businessmen, and former Kuomintang members committed suicide. Their lives disappeared like droplets of water evaporating in the air. No memorial services were given for those people who died because suicide was a crime.

In 1968, there was another movement to send the students and city residents to the countryside, which was to serve as "universities" to be "re-educated by the poor and lower-middle-class peasants." Many of the city residents did not want to go but had no choice, so they left their children alone in the city. Those that were too young, they brought with them.

My mother did not get a result from the highest authority in the province. Instead, they suggested that she should follow Mao's direction: "Go to the vastness of the countryside, there are plenty of opportunities for one's talents." My mother had already gone to her parents' hometown in the countryside. Yet she found out her stay there was not legitimate, either. When she asked the leader of her village to assign her a job, she was rejected.

There were seven villages in our hometown. After the Land Reform movement, each village formed a collective farm, and later it became a "production team" of the people's commune in 1958. The seven production teams formed a brigade, and a few brigades formed a commune.

The production team leader could not assign my mother any job because to work in the production team and get paid, one must be a member of the commune. My mother left her hometown before the commune was formed. Typically, a woman who left the village to get married was no longer considered a member of the village. The village leader had to hold a village-wide meeting to discuss if my mother could become a member. The villagers had many arguments about accepting my mother. There was a big argument between the two sides in a meeting. One side felt my mother was very pitiful and deserved to work.

A man jumped up. "We don't want to add three more people to the production team to share our grain."

One of my grandaunts said, "She was born here. She deserves to join the commune."

A woman who was a poor peasant immediately yelled, "We don't want any bad elements to join our commune."

Another young woman added, "She and her family are the counter-revolutionaries. They are the enemies of the people."

The worst was my fourth aunt-in-law, the one that villagers called "shot-dead-ghost's daughter." She pointed a finger at my mother's nose and yelled, "Don't you feel shame? You are a married woman. You should join your husband's commune. A good daughter would not come back to her parents' home." This pushed my mother into an emotional hell. She could only cry. But because she had cried so much in recent years, her tears had dried up.

Jealousy caused my aunt-in-law to dislike my mother. When she had given birth to her son Tian ten days before my birth in 1964, her mother could not help her because her mother had the counter-revolutionary title. My grandmother took care of her and her son for only ten days. When I was born, my grandma left them and came to the city to care for me. After that, my aunt-in-law hated my grandmother, my mother, and me. She did not know how difficult life was for us without food and money in the city. My father was already in the labor camp before my birth. My aunt-in-law thought that her son should be more important than me because her son was from a son's side of the family, and I was from the daughter's side.

The leader did not assign any job to my mother, but my mother still went out to work with other villagers without pay. While she was working with the villagers, they treated her like the plague, and everybody walked away from her. The three of us became aliens; we did not belong to the city or the countryside. There was no place for us in society!

During this time, we were financially supported by my grandparents. They managed it by selling their house in the city during our most difficult time. The house was co-owned by their two other brothers. My grandparents divided the sale proceeds—three thousand yuan—among the granduncles. My grandparents used their portion of the money to buy food from the black market to feed the three of us. At that time, buying and selling things from the black markets was illegal. Authorities could confiscate everything if they got caught. Since we didn't have resident permits, and thus no food coupons, we had no choice but to risk paying a high price to get food from the black market. Sometimes, I saw my aunts and hard of hearing uncle move something secretly from a small boat to the house after dark. I was curious and ran to the house to see what kind of stuff was. When I opened the bags, there were sweet potatoes and broken rice that Po Po had brought from the black market. The broken rice was cheaper. When my fourth uncle and aunt-in-law found out, they were angry with my grandmother and said, "Family wealth cannot be distributed to a daughter." My grandmother had no choice but gave them two hundred yuan because she did not want them to leak the secret to outsiders.

My mother was so worried that we might not survive if we continued to live without being legal residents in the commune. Also, my sister was already nine years old and still could not go to school because we had no legal status to live there. My mother went to the local county authority in her hometown numerous times to request legal resident status in the commune. The last time she went to the local county office with us, she brought a mosquito net and an old comforter. She planned to sleep in front of the local office if they did not register her in the commune. She talked to the head officer, Mr. Wanwang Luo. She said, "Guangzhou City would not issue residence permits for the three of us, couldn't my hometown admit us? Where do we belong?" She added: "If you are not going to issue the legal resident status to us today, then my children and I are not going to leave, and the three of us will die in front of your office."

Mr. Wanwang Luo seemed not to care and said: "There is nothing I can do. You should go home." At the end of the day, he walked out of his office and found the three of us still sitting there. He hesitated and talked to my mother and told my mother again to go home. While they were talking, I cried for food, and it triggered my sister to weep quietly. Mr. Wanwang Luo showed a hint of sympathy, and he offered to help us. He rode his bike to the village to investigate the whole case, and then he put great pressure on the commune's leaders and ordered them to give legal resident status to the three of us. He threatened the commune's leaders: If they did not comply, he would charge them for going against Chairman Mao's orders!

It was 1971. We finally got the household registered in the countryside commune. The three of us, at last, had a place to settle down and the right to work and go to school. The county head also ordered the local office to issue the grain ration to us. In the countryside, instead of issuing food coupons, the commune distributed grain to each commune member. However, it was not the rice harvest time, so there was no grain left in the local commune to give to us. That was a problem for the village leaders, so they borrowed some grain from some of the peasants who had a little extra and gave it to my mother.

My mother still remembers Mr. Wanwang Luo; she appreciated what he did for her. She had spent so much time in the highest authority in Guangzhou City and so much time in her county, but no one had helped her except Wanwang Luo, who lent a hand to her when she was practically drowning in despair. There were always some nice people who had compassion and moral integrity in their hearts.

Finally, my sister and I were able to go to school, and my mother was able to earn a little salary when she went to work. The three of us were featured in a local newspaper, which stated that we listened to Chairman Mao's directive to go to the countryside, "to the vastness of the countryside, there is plenty of scope for one's talents. . . ." My mother suddenly became a model citizen in the city. In those days, no one wanted to live in the countryside because there were fewer educational opportunities, and the standard of living was much lower than in the city. Of course, the news was propaganda. We went to the countryside because we had no other choice.

CHAPTER 13

A WILD COUNTRYSIDE GIRL

MY GRANDMA USUALLY WOKE UP early in the morning and used her net to catch some small fish and shrimp from the canal. The fish in the ponds belonged to the commune; no one was allowed to catch them. Her net was attached to a long bamboo stick, so she did not have to get into the water to catch the fish and shrimp. She always took out the big ones around two inches long to preserve them with a lot of salt and left the smaller ones, like an inch long, for dinner. Therefore, we sometimes had a little salt fish for our meals. By the time I was around six or seven years old, I had become an expert at catching fish and shrimp by myself. Whenever I saw that the tide was very low, I would find the area of the canal populated by fish. I would ask others, who were usually older than me, to help because of the sheer size of the job and the limited time before high tide. I had to dry that section of the canal within a few hours before the high tide. First, we would dig in the mud to make two little barriers and made sure the dikes were strong enough to block the water. Then we used the washbasins to scoop the water out from the blocked section. We did this until the area was dry. If we were lucky, we could get one to two pounds of small fish, shrimp, and clams from the bottom. Sometimes the dike was not strong enough, and the water washed in. Whenever a little water leaked from the barrier, someone would use his body to block the water from coming in. The others would then try to catch the fish as quickly as possible before the muddy barrier totally collapsed.

When I was six years old, my mother finally got our residence permits, and then she asked her brothers, sisters, and their children to help her to build a small house behind my second uncle's house next to the canal. We called him Second Uncle. He assigned different duties to my cousins; then he got on a small boat to get the mud from the canal, which was the material to build the walls of the house. My hard of hearing uncle cut the bamboo from Po Po's yard. My aunts brought the straw and fastened them together. My oldest cousin, the son of Big Uncle, was the most talented man in the village. He used a small string to measure the ground and directed other cousins to dig the foundation. My mother went to prepare lunch for the helpers. A kind, middle-aged man came to help. He just said hello to my cousins then picked up the bamboo to make the framing for the walls of the house. The framing was a grid of vertical and horizontal bamboo.

Po Po came and said, "Thanks for coming to help. How are you doing these days?"

The man replied, "I am fine. You are building a house for Ah Zhen. Why didn't you tell me?"

"Oh, we can finish the job by ourselves. The house is a small one."

"I will feel guilty if I don't help. You helped me so much when I was young."

This man, Gu, was a former farm laborer of my grandparents in the old days. Soon Second Uncle came back with a boat of mud. When he saw Gu, he was very excited and said, "Gu, I can't believe you are here!" Then they started to chat with each other.

The next day, the bamboo framing was done. My aunts and my mother were busy mixing the straw with mud to form a square piece like a small carpet; my cousins picked up the role of creating a straw-mud carpet and hung it on the horizontal lines of bamboo of the frame. It took a day to build the wall because the mud straw was very heavy. Everybody was very tired, and my mother brought a few dishes out and asked them to eat; they gobbled the food in a few minutes, even it was only vegetables and dry, small, salt fish.

On the third day, the mud was still wet but eventually would be dry, so all the pieces were glued together to form the walls. Gu came again in the early morning to help. A few men worked together to hang a wood beam on top of the walls to form a thatched roof by attaching bamboo with the beam. My cousins used a ladder to bring the clipped straw onto the roof. Gu and Second Uncle were already on top; they both put the straw on, layer after layer neatly, and tied it onto the roof. I was very happy to see the new mud-straw house being completed, and I saw everyone was smiling at their accomplishment.

My fourth uncle stopped by and said, "What a crappy mud house! This family will never have a chance to turn itself around!" He did not like us because his wife always hated us and hated my Po Po.

Gu said, "How can you predict anything in the future? Dry oil can pop out a fire if it has the right chance." My uncle left bitterly. Everybody cheered Gu. Gu said to my mother, "Don't be upset with that villain."

A very small one-room house with mud walls stood on one-eighth acre of land next to the canal. Once the mud wall dried, a person brought a bucket with white paint and a big brush to write in big words LONG LIVE CHAIRMAN MAO! on the wall facing the street. I did not feel the wall was ugly at all; instead, I was happy and proud. I used to

see these kinds of words on all the houses, such as SAIL-
ING THE SEA DEPENDS ON THE HELMSMAN, WAGING
REVOLUTION DEPENDS ON MAO ZEDONG'S THOUGHTS!
SMASH THE FOUR OLDS! These slogans became part of
everyday speech and were even considered fashionable
statements.

The east side of our house had a big pond, and behind
the pond was an orchard. They had belonged to my grandparents before the communist land reform. On the west
side of our house were the canal, bamboo, and trees that
grew neatly on both sides of the canal. Less than a half
mile from our house was the Pearl River, where a huge levee was built to protect the village from floods. This house
was like ancient, primitive housing with no electricity, city
water, or a single modern building material. But it had a
good natural environment, not only for the people but
also for the farm animals. From then on, we moved out of
my grandma's house and had our own house. I was able to
raise a few animals like I wanted.

Summer days in the countryside were the happiest
and fairest days of the year. In the afternoon, we often
would spend hours playing in the water. We played different kinds of water games. When the waves weren't as big
as we wanted, two kids would climb on a boat and shake
it vigorously. Other kids swam with the waves. Sometimes
after they waded for a while, we turned the boat upside
down, and all of us got inside the flipped boat. We laughed
and sang. The adults sat on the shore under the bamboo
trees gossiping; some of them made baskets or furniture
from bamboo. For safety, one or two of the elders always
watched us from a distance.

At night in the countryside, the moonlight reflected the image of trees and bamboo on houses' walls. The

bamboo swayed harmoniously with the wind, and the insects' singing resonated with the sound of rustling leaves. The night became crowded with sound if one listened quietly. There was no electricity in our house; blackness swallowed everything when there was no moonlight. I could not see my fingers in front of my eyes, so I was scared to walk out. We only had a small kerosene light that shimmered in the house. As a child, I always appreciated the moon. I believed there was a fairy that lived up there.

The fifteenth day of the lunar month was the full moon. The moonlight would shine down its watery, white-silver glow onto the village, illuminating everything. It shone on the canal like glowing fish scales' band of silver, both sides of the canal bustling with noise, especially in the lunar month of August, which has the brightest night of the whole year; it was when all the family reunions were held. People came out to sing the local traditional water songs. This was a competition in which people had to create instant lyrics with questions and answers for each other.

Sometimes, one of the singers would sound out one sentence of a famous poem from a thousand years ago and ask another one to answer the next sentence of that poem. Ruen's mother was an excellent singer in our village. She was also an excellent composer. Ruen got her DNA; he became a very good singer in the village. The kids were excited; we cheered our singers, who competed with neighboring village singers. We made sweet and sour papaya for the singers so they would not dry their throats due to the length of time they spent singing. Some of those songs were still ringing in my ears many years after I left my home village.

Every lunar month of May Fifth was a big holiday for the village people because we had a dragon boat race festival. Each production team would have about five to six boats to race. We had seven production teams in our brigade, so there were around forty boats to join in the competition. Each boat held a small boy; his job was to scoop the water out while the boat drew water during the competition. Any boat that won the first prize would get a whole roast pig. One year, one of the boats in our production team won the first prize; everybody was happy and full of pride. By the time they wanted to claim the prize, the leaders of the brigade had said that they had no right to get the prize because there was a son of a landlord in that boat. The competitors in the same boat also could not get a prize because the son of the landlord had let them down.

My childhood was a mix of happiness and fear but mostly fear. Living close to the waterfront was beautiful, but people had to watch out for water during flood season. I had seen floods knock down a brick factory outside of the levee in a second. One summer evening, people ran to the levee; I ran there with other children. Once I got up there, it was unbelievable that the river had expanded so much. It looked like a sea to me: brownish-colored water flowed furiously to the east; all the vegetation and trees outside of the levee had been swamped. Leaders of the village measured the level of water every hour. They wanted to see how many inches were left before the water would reach the top of the levee. All the adults were gravely concerned, and I could see the fear in their eyes. They told the kids to go home, but I was the only child who was reluctant to go since I did not know the danger of flooding. As I stood on top of the levee, I felt like I was on top of the Earth. The ferocious flood flying down the river was a magnificent picture for me. I stood there for an hour before I went back home.

That night I had a good sleep. When I woke up, I heard that the village leaders and some adults didn't sleep the whole night. People gossiped about somewhere far away from where a levee had been destroyed by a flood, and many people had died. Some of the bodies still held on to something like sugar canes or tree branches after they were dead. *Dong, dong, dong*, the sound of the production team's bell vibrated throughout the village; all the laborers rushed to the office. The leaders announced the destruction from the flood, and they ordered all the laborers to the disaster area to combat the flood. My mother left my sister and me without telling me. She was gone more than a week. I stayed home as usual; the village was strangely quiet.

While my mother was away, my grandmother came every night to cajole my sister and me to sleep. She tucked our quilts around us, then always told us to be good children for my mother and have sweet dreams. I fell asleep while she was petting me. Slowly, the voice of my grandma became my aunts' voices. I sat on a small boat with my three aunts, who paddled hard against the turbulent waves. There were so many people paddling their boats like us. Water had swamped all the houses and trees, and terrifying waves, each one larger than the one before, crashed into everything on the water. The surging waves were like a monster who tossed the boats as if they were toys. Suddenly, all the boats flipped, and people were screaming. My three aunts' heads appeared on the water. I tried to catch them. One of my aunts yelled, "Ah Jade, come, come to me." I spent all my energy swimming toward her and yelled, "Aunt! Aunt!" but they flowed farther away.

"Wake up! Ah Jade, wake up!"

I woke up and saw my sister. My sister said, "You had a nightmare. Don't worry, I am here with you." The house was extremely quiet. I asked where Grandma was; she said that my grandmother had other things to do, so she could not sleep with us.

In the morning, I ran up to the levee to look. The flood had gone down; the leaves of the trees emerged from the water at the outside of the levee. My mother came back, and she was excited to see us. We asked her some questions about the place she had gone to, but she did not tell us a word.

As the water almost went back to the normal level, water still covered the fields in a shallow pond, and many very small streams had a lot of fish and shrimp in them. There were different kinds of fish; some of them were weird looking, like pufferfish. We poked around them because they could expand their bodies like balls. The adults warned us not to touch them because they were toxic and dangerous, but we were fearless as long as we had fun. The shrimp were much bigger than the ones we saw in the ponds. Everybody in the village except the laborers went there to catch fish. I got there early since my house was close to the levee. I tried to build a dike to block a section of a stream so I could catch the fish. Once I built the dike, I claimed that a portion of the stream, and I did not allow others to catch my fish. While I was building the dike, my older cousin came and tried to help me. He used his shovel to make the dike stronger. Suddenly, village security came, and without any explanation, grabbed the shovel away from my older cousin and walked away. My cousin ran to take it, but the security man acted as if he had unlimited power. He said that my cousin was supposed to use the shovel to work in the field, not to catch fish. Some people stood up and stopped catching fish. They encouraged my cousin to get the shovel back, but my cousin did not have the nerve. At that moment, I saw my hard of hearing and mute uncle, who was also watching. I rushed in front of him and made gestures to ask him to get the shovel back. He hesitated a bit and then chased the security guy like a maniac. All the people stood up and watched. Some people started to cheer, and others responded. Suddenly, they were cheering up like crazy. They shouted, "Catch him! Catch that bad guy from hell! Get the shovel back!" Soon the security man ran to the top of the levee and blew his whistle, but my uncle could not hear; he still chased him. The security man dropped the shovel and ran away. Everybody was wild with joy like it was a carnival. My uncle's actions relieved their anger because the village security man was always arrogant and lazy. Best of all, no one could accuse my uncle of disobeying the authorities because he was a hard of hearing mute man.

Chapter 14

WORKING FOR A POINT SYSTEM

In the countryside commune, the peasants had to work on a point system (see Appendix C) to earn rice and money. In addition, one resident received a coupon for two feet and six inches of fabric each year. This length of fabric was enough to make only underwear. Therefore, the people saved the fabric coupons for a few years to make pants or a shirt. The sugar allotment was four Liang per person per month; kerosene for lamp light was one Liang per person per month. There was even a coupon for buying matches.

The production team distributed a small amount of fish to each resident a few times a year on holidays like Chinese New Year. Usually a half-pound for a kid and one pound for an adult. Those were the only times that the villagers had big fish to eat since most big fish had to export to Hong Kong. Those fish were not free; they cost 0.40 yuan per pound; villagers needed to use working points to buy them. The lowest level of labor force only earned 0.10 yuan per day. A regular working man could make up to 0.27 yuan per day. My mother earned 0.13 yuan per day. The leaders made much more than 0.50 yuan per day.

When we had big fish for our meal, I would pick up the best part of the fish and ask my grandmother, "Is this piece what Chairman Mao would eat?" My grandmother did not say anything, but my mother would reply, "Just eat your fish, and don't talk."

When my mother received a resident permit back

from her birth village, she finally had a job to work on the point system like other peasants. I remembered the first day she went to work. She woke up my sister and me very early in the morning and said: "From now on, I need to go to work in the production team every day. You will need to learn to prepare and cook lunch and dinner."

"Okay, I know how to start the fire and cook the rice in the ceramic pot," my sister replied.

"Me too! I can start the fire!" I added. I thought making fire was fun, and I used to watch adults do it in the kitchen. I was six years old at that time. The sky was barely light; my mother took a shovel, walked out, and quickly disappeared in the morning fog.

At the village's production team meeting, the team leader announced that my mother was becoming a new member of the team. The leader told my mother, "You should report to work at the side of the fishpond tomorrow." My mother was happy because she could again earn money and food. When she happily reported to work on the first day, she saw only about ten strong men there with the team leader.

My mother asked the leader: "What is my assignment?"

He pointed to a small boat next to the fishpond: "Dig the mud from the fishpond's bottom,

scoop it onto the boat, and haul it to the paddy fields for fertilizer." He explained, "The mud holds a lot of nutrients, and the rice grows very well from it."

It was a very tough job because she had to pull the boat filled with heavy mud from the fishponds to the paddy field. This was not a job a woman could handle. Obviously, the leader purposely gave her a hard time because he did not want to give my mother a job, but he had to obey his superior to give her one. My mother did not say anything; she pulled the mud from one location to another and spread it out on top of the field. The little water in the rice field could not float the boat, and my mother did not have the strength to drag it, so she asked my nine-year-old sister to help her to push the boat while my mother pulled it with a rope. My sister was very skinny and short; the mud would submerge half of her small body since the paddy field itself was immersed in at least a foot of mud. While pulling the boat, she looked at a bleak paddy field without another woman working there, only a dozen men working silently. She once again looked back to see her daughter pushing the boat for her. "What an innocent girl. She should be playing with other children, not working in the field with me." To my mother's desolate mental state, volatile emotions were added. Every step was grueling for my sister as well as my mother. After a day of arduous work, they were exhausted and hungry. Therefore, making meals became my responsibility as a six year old.

Cooking dinner was not easy at that time. There was no gas or electric stove like in modern days. We didn't even have coal or firewood as cooking fuel in our village. We had to burn leaves and small branches to make a fire. So my first job was to collect the leaves that had fallen on the ground from all kinds of trees and dry grass around the village. Then I had to start a fire in the brick stove using those leaves. The stove was made by my mother, who used mud to glue the bricks together. On sunny days, it was easy to light the dry leaves. On rainy days, however, it was very difficult since the leaves were wet. Our area is subtropical to the tropical coastal area, and there are about one-hundred-forty to one-hundred-sixty rainy days per year. All too often, I created smoke but no fire. The heavy smoke choked me; my eyes filled with tears. In that case, worry and fear also built up, which caused me anxiety. I knew if I could not start the fire, we would not be able to eat anything, and my mother would blame me, so I had to blow harder and harder on it for a long time, hoping the fire would start.

My mother used to send my sister to come back earlier to help me because she knew that I was too young to do the cooking alone. One early evening, I was using a ceramic pot for cooking rice. Suddenly, the bottom of the pot broke, and all the rice dropped on the stove. I was nervous because I had wasted rice. My sister came back in time after work; she saw me in a state of utter stupefaction; I did not know what to do. She hurried to scoop the rice out from the stove, then washed it carefully and made sure all fire ash cleaned out, and she also filtered out the sand from the rice. Next, she transferred the rice into a wok to cook it again, but damp leaves plus wet stove only produced a lot of smoke. We could not get them to start a fire even though we blew and blew. I was too exhausted to blow, and I tried to light another match.

My sister stopped me. "Don't use too many matches. We have used up the matches coupon this month."

After we finished the cooking, our eyes were still feeling the burn from the smoke. My mother came back from work, and she noticed my sister's pants were still wet with mud stuck on. She said, "Why didn't you change your pants? It is easy to catch a cold." My sister went to change her clothing. My mother walked to the kitchen, and I followed behind her. I was worried that she might blame me for breaking the pot. I ran in front of her and said, "Mama, the pot broke. I didn't do it. It broke by itself." She looked at the pot and raised her head, looked at me, then made a sound that was something between a sigh and forgiveness. A few days later, my mother purchased another ceramic pot, but this time she wrapped iron wire tightly around the pot; that way, the bottom of the pot would not break again.

My mother worked on this mud dredging assignment for a few weeks, seven days a week. The production team leader was surprised that she could handle it for so long. After this assignment, he assigned her different kinds of heavy duty jobs for about a year. Later, when some villagers gossiped that the leader was so cruel, he changed my mother's assignment to some regular woman's jobs. One was to cut grass to feed the fish in the ponds. The grass was the main food for the fish. My mother had to cut at least a hundred pounds to get the points she needed. That much grass was not easy to find because the farmers used every inch of soil to plant something edible like grain, fruit trees, and vegetables. Once my mother got this assignment, she had to search for grass around the edges of the paddy fields, the edges of the fishponds, or the sides of the roads. In the afternoon, she would put all the grass in two baskets she had prepared and carry them to the production team to be weighed. It was too hot; her shirt was soaked with perspiration. She felt the heat blistering the soles of her feet with every excruciating step because she had no shoes on. She walked as fast as she could to avoid burning her feet. The exhausting labor combined with the humiliation and the grave tension finally took a toll on my mother. She collapsed with a painful stomach, but she had no money to seek medical treatment. She still had to go to work in this condition.

Even with those hard jobs, my mother could not earn enough points to get enough grain to feed the family of three because she was in the fourth level of the labor force, and she earned around three points per day, one point was equivalent to 0.03 to 0.04 yuan. Sometimes she helped other villagers make clothing at night in exchange for points. With the extra work and occasional small amount of money my father sent to us, my mother could buy food in the black market without the ration coupons, and she was just barely able to make it. The price with and without the coupons was very different. For example, a pound of rice with a coupon was 0.14 yuan, and without a ration, the rice was 0.75–1.00 yuan per pound.

In addition to the point system, each family among the countryside residents received "self-retained land" granted from the government. Ninety-three percent of farmland belonged to the commune, and the remaining seven percent of the farmland was divided among each family depending on how many members were in the family. The "self-retained land" was for each family to grow their own vegetables, peanuts, and beans. My family had about 0.2 acres of self-retained land, which was why the villagers were not happy when my mother received a residence permit in the countryside because we would share the small number of resources like self-retained land and grain with them. Also, the production team leader had to assign a job to my mother that allowed her to earn points, which diluted their resources.

My countryside had very rich soil. We grew plenty of rice, sugarcane, peanuts, and litchi. We also raised a lot of fish. But we barely had enough food because, after the harvest, almost the entire crop went to the government. Some of the products like litchi had to be handed over almost entirely to the collective. That was because the government sold a lot of these products to Hong Kong to get foreign currency. Each night around nine or ten o'clock,

I heard ship engines passing by the Pearl River. By the next day afternoon, those cargo ships came back. I liked to count those ships; these were nine ships each day; they seemed to move slowly on the river. One time I was walking on top of the levee; I tried to compete with the cargo ship to see who could go faster. But no matter how I ran, I could not catch up with the ships. I realized that the ship moved much faster than it looked because of the distance. When I was a child, there were so many litchi trees. This fruit grew once a year, depending on the variety. One variety ripened at the end of spring, and another one ripened in the summer; they were beautiful. When we looked at the shiny red litchi fruit, our mouths filled with saliva, we could easily pick the litchis by just raising our hands even though we were very short, but we did not have the courage. In that time of scarcity, most people ascribed to the moral dictate that anything belonging to the public should not be touched. But as little kids, we could not resist the temptation, and when we got the opportunity, we secretly picked one to eat. Anyone caught by public security was punished severely. Each person, even the children, had to pay one yuan for each fruit. The average peasant salary at the time was seven to nine yuan per month for the strong men and women of good status, which was equivalent to about four US dollars. My mother earned only about four yuan per month.

Because of the moral issue and the fine, no one had the nerve to pick the litchis. On harvesting day, many boats parked in the canal to carry the fruit to the cargo ships parked on Pearl River. The ships carried the fruit to Hong Kong the same day.

Our food depended on the natural resources of the coastal waters, and we had better opportunities for earning more points than other places because of the rich soil. One particular way to earn more points was collecting mud from fishponds to make potting soil. Every early spring, to collect more points fast, all families, including the children, came out to be part of the workforce. The production team leaders first sent the strong peasants to collect the mud from the fishpond. The mud was left on the field to dry for a few weeks. Once the mud became clay, then we cut the clay into small cubes in half-inch squares so we could weigh them. The weight determined the points we earned. The production team exported the clay cubes as potting soil to Hong Kong according to the economic plan of the government. Even with all this effort, our villagers had barely enough to survive, but it was still better than in many parts of China at that time.

CHAPTER 15

A SCHOOL WITHOUT CLASSROOMS

AFTER WE OBTAINED OUR RESIDENT PERMIT in our home village, we finally had the right to go to school. My sister was already nine years old when she went to elementary school for the first time. At that time, kids started elementary school at seven years old. I was not yet seven. I remember how exciting it was on her first day at school. We woke up early that morning when the village's loudspeaker played every day's first song "The east is red, the sun is rising. From China appears Mao Zedong, He strives for the people's happiness, Hurrah, he is the people's great savior!" My mother had already made rice porridge breakfast for us. After eating, my sister and I rushed to get our new bookbags and pencils. The bookbags were made by my mother the day before using small leftover fabric stitched together; the centerpiece of fabric had beautiful flowers.

After my mother made the bag for my sister, I begged my mother: "Make one for me, too! I want to go to school, too!"

My mom said, "You are not seven yet. You will go to school next year."

"No, no, I want to go now. I want a book bag, too!" So my mother made a bookbag for me that was smaller than my sister's; it could barely hold a notebook and a pencil.

My sister proudly carried her book bag on her shoulder and walked out of the house, headed to the school. I quickly followed her. We arrived at the school. It was just a few small mud houses with flat ground in front. My sister found the first grade classroom. She said to me: "You have to stay outside because you are not a student in this class." Since I always listened to my sister, I stood outside of a window and watched inside. There was no glass on the windows, which were just a few big holes on the mud wall, so I could see and hear everything. There were three rows of tables with benches; each row was lined with eight tables; each table had one bench that two students could sit on. A picture of Chairman Mao hung on top of the blackboard. A lot of students were already inside of the classroom and talking. My sister stood in front of the classroom and seemed to be taller than all the other kids since she was two years older than they. Soon the bell rang. All the students found their desks and sat down, except my sister, who still stood where she was.

A young female teacher in her early twenties walked into the classroom. She was Ms. Yang, one of the city's "educated youths" sent to our countryside by Mao's call during the Cultural Revolution. I noticed that she looked so different than the local people. Most people wore the same style green or dark blue clothes, and she wore light blue, high-waisted, foreign style clothing.

Once she stood in front of the class, a student leader stood up and shouted, "Stand up!"

Then the whole class stood straight as bamboo and shouted, "Study hard and advance every day!" It was a quote from Mao.

The teacher said: "Sit down!" and looked at my sister. "This is your new classmate, Chan Sue." She pointed to an empty seat in the back row. My sister walked to that seat and sat down. The class started. The teacher wrote a short sentence on the blackboard and read it, and then, she asked the students to repeat it loudly. I followed them and shouted the sentence, stuttering.

The teacher noticed me standing outside and said: "Who is that girl?"

My sister's face turned red, and she said, "Teacher, she is my younger sister."

Ms. Yang called me to come in and asked, "What is your name? How old are you?" I walked in and said: "I am A...h Jade, I am...six years old."

She smiled at me and said, "You can sit next to your sister." I was so happy that my heart leapt. From then on, I became a "student." I felt so relaxed in her classroom. Unfortunately, I could not stay in her class for the following year in second grade because I had to start my official first grade student year in another class.

Elementary school was supposed to teach the kids to learn how to read, write Chinese, learn math, and gain general knowledge. But during the Cultural Revolution, the school's primary objective became to learn Mao Zedong's thoughts. One of the first-grade lessons we studied was "Great leader Chairman Mao taught us: The core force to lead our mission is the Chinese Communist Party. The theoretical foundation to guide our thought is Marxism and Leninist." I could memorize and recite all those lessons, but as a first grader I had absolutely no clue what they meant.

During the Cultural Revolution, the school followed Chairman Mao's instruction to "combine education with practical experience." Students above third grade were sent to work in the fields instead of studying in the classroom. Our school required students to work at least two full days every week or sometimes every half day for a whole month. We attended school in the morning and worked in the afternoon. The student was required to bring work tools, such as a shovel or a hoe, but my family only had one shovel and one hoe since we moved there from the city. My mother did not have any money to buy extra tools for me. When my mother took one to work, my sister took another one, so I had nothing to bring to school. Therefore, I was usually criticized by my teacher, Mr. Gao, in front of the whole class for not bringing a tool.

One time, we were assigned a one-month job moving soil from one place to another. Since I didn't have a shovel, I was assigned to transport the soil by holding a wooden pole on my right shoulder with two dangling baskets of soil hanging on each side. After a half day, my shoulder was covered in painful bruises. But I had to keep working to avoid criticism from my teacher. In school, the teacher always taught us that getting used to tough conditions was good experience. But I did not feel these hard conditions were good for me because my right shoulder was very painful. I was only in elementary school, not yet strong enough to do this job. The following working day, I rotated the burden of soil to my left shoulder since my right shoulder was still covered with bruises from the previous day, but my left shoulder was not as strong as the right one. Mr. Gao saw that I had difficulty moving the soil with two baskets swinging loosely on my wobbly legs, so he assigned another small student to help me. The two of us used one wooden pole to hold one basket of soil. Even with help, I could barely make it. Mr. Gao always held a short meeting following the end of the workday to evaluate each student's performance, and each day he pointed to me:

"You didn't bring a tool again. Make sure you bring one tomorrow!"

I was so ashamed. I could not tell him that I didn't have

one because my family was so poor. I tried everything to prevent the teacher from criticizing me. I humbly always worked harder. One time I took a hoe that was hidden behind a door in my Second Uncle's house, and I was so happy to be able to bring a tool to school. While I was using the hoe to make my first dig in the field, the metal blade flew off the handle. The whole class screamed, "Watch out!" The vice principal saw it and said, "Are you trying to kill someone?" I did not say anything; I was scared to death. From that day on, I steeled myself to go to school without a tool.

Once, the school sent us to dig sweet potatoes. Since I did not have a hoe or shovel, I helped the other students collect the sweet potatoes after digging them out of the ground. My classmates were very happy I could help them. I'd pick up the sweet potatoes as fast as I could and gathered the sweet potatoes vines, using a rope to tie them nicely so that the students could bring the vines to the fishponds. Nonetheless, the vice principal saw me and criticized me. "Why don't you dig yourself instead of fooling around!" I felt that I worked so hard to help so many classmates. But without a tool, I could not do the digging part, and it became my fault. I swallowed my tears into my heart. Every student had a tool but me.

In school as well as at home, we read and learned from the Cultural Revolution propaganda books. Children's comics were illustrated propaganda stories about the revolutionary heroes, the suppression of bad landlords, and saving poor people by the communists from the old society. All other books were considered poison to the new society. There were many stories about children turning against their grandparents and parents because they were performing suspicious activities against the government.

Those books also described that the landlords never gave up their wish to overthrow the new society. When I read those picture books, I believed the communists were doing all good for us.

On the other hand, I would not turn against my family because I thought my mother and grandmother were most important to me. In those days, everyone was very poor, but every household had to buy the four-volume set of *The Select Works of Mao Zedong* to study every day. Many families did not want to be accused of being disloyal, so they bought the set, even if they did not have money to buy food. My mother did not buy Chairman Mao's books. Instead, she bought a dictionary. She reasoned that she had to learn how to read first before reading Chairman Mao's book. I was so happy that I had a dictionary; I read that dictionary for days because we did not have any other interesting books to read except the propaganda books.

The vice principal was prejudiced against me because I was the daughter of a "class enemy." He sometimes repeated a cliché, "A dragon is born of a dragon, a phoenix is born of a phoenix, and a mouse is born with the ability to make a hole." In a nutshell, since the parents were class enemies, the children would naturally be bad elements, too.

My teacher Mr. Gao liked to flatter the village leaders. He always chose student leaders from kids whose parents were village leaders. One time, he walked into the classroom and announced that our class needed a new student leader. We immediately had a few outstanding classmates in our minds and thought Mr. Gao would choose one of them. It was unbelievable that he named a student who was the worst one in the class, a complete jerk. We were so shocked and could not believe our ears. Mr. Gao sensed that his students disagreed with him, so he repeated the new leader's name word by word. We looked at each other and burst out laughing. Mr. Gao stood up and explained to us that the student he had chosen had made significant improvement, and we should encourage him instead of laughing. Mr. Gao said most importantly, the new leader was the most conscious of the class system in communist China. This student leader had the worst academic grades in the class.

Grades were not as important as having the "correct thoughts," which meant we all had to abide by this ideology. In late 1972, a student named Zhang Tiesheng was promoted as a national model student, but his academic test score was zero. Similarly, in 1973, a fifth grade girl named Huang Shui wrote an article for the Beijing newspaper. In her article, she questioned, "Are we, the young people of the Mao Zedong era, still slaves of teacher's authority under the old education system?" For a time, she became a hero figure for all the students in the country. Learning her article became our school lesson. Mr. Gao assigned memorizing every word of her article as homework. I did not understand a word of what she wrote because I was too young to understand politics. The article had no meaning at all, but I was always afraid of Mr. Gao; therefore, I woke up at 4:30 A.M. to cram that article.

In contrast, Mr. Gao's wife Ms. Yang was my favorite teacher. I had her before I became an official student, and one year when I was in middle school, and she treated me very well. My sister had her for five years in elementary school. Ms. Yang made my sister the leader of the whole school for a few years. Ms. Yang used to wear beautiful, stylish clothing from Hong Kong. Some people said that her relatives were either in Hong Kong or in America. I always admired her clothing; I wished I had some like hers, but often I heard some people would say, "She dresses in a bourgeoisie style." I had no idea they were jealous or hated her clothing. She was a strict teacher and did not care about a student's family background. I remember that one day she came to my first grade class because my regular teacher was absent. A student's mother, who was a leader in the village, brought a bowl of sugar egg custard to the classroom and said, "Ms. Yang, my son needs nutrition, he didn't eat much this morning." Without Ms. Yang's permission, she came in and put the bowl on her son's desk. All the students watched the bowl with open eyes because none of us had sugar egg custard for breakfast every day. I thought, *If I had sugar egg custard once a year, I would be thrilled.* Ms. Yang could not tolerate this; she yelled loudly in front of the whole class. "How can my students learn anything in my class like this? Next time, if you bring egg custard to the class, you need to bring it for all the students!" We were surprised that Ms. Yang spoke out because my regular teacher just let the mother bring breakfast into the classroom almost every morning without a complaint.

Being able to join school activities was the most desired goal for the students. The activities were usually related to ideas that promoted the revolutionization of children's minds. Like most children, I wanted to join, but I was left out because of my family's label or maybe because of my hunchback. One time our school had an activity to learn the military salute and the walk for the military parade. This time, the teacher Mr. Gao included me in the team because he needed more students. I was extremely happy that I could join the team. The teacher put me behind the other classmates, but I did not mind. While I was walking in line in the sports field, I tried to stand straight and hide my hunched back so I could look like a soldier. I was so proud; there were no words to describe how happy I was. Suddenly, my old right shoe cracked open and flew to the front of the line. The whole team immediately stopped, and everybody looked back. The two classmates next to me burst out laughing. I felt so embarrassed. Mr. Gao immediately stopped us and dismissed me as well as the other two students who had laughed at me. I was despondent and felt guilty to have let down those two classmates.

I also did not have a pair of decent pants to wear. Usually, there were a few patches in front of my knees. One day, the needle thread of the inner stitching was loose. The hole became bigger and bigger and spread to the crotch of the trousers. It was awful. I tried not to move around in the classroom, but there was gym class that day. I was scared to tell the teacher that I could not go because I did not want the whole class to know. I walked like I was holding urine so that nobody would see the hole in my pants.

After school, I went back home and got a needle to patch it up, very carefully stitch by stitch for an hour. Finally, the pants were repaired. I smiled, "Yay, I have pants to wear." But when I tried to wear them, my leg could not get through because I had stitched both sides of the pant tube together. I tried to patch it again, but the fabric was too old and fragile; it could not hold together anymore. I sat there, clutching my pants, weeping. Just in time, my mother came back from work. Seeing her, I started to cry loudly.

"Why are you crying?" my mother asked.

"I don't have pants to wear to go to school!" I wiped my eyes.

My mother took a look at my pants, and she let out a sigh.

"They are too old. I am going to make new ones for you."

I was skeptical because I always wore the pants passed down from my sister. I saw my mother open a small bag that had a fabric coupon in it and then she walked out. The next morning when I woke up, I saw new black pants on top of my bed. I was so excited! That was the first time I wore new pants. I immediately tried them on; they were short, barely covering my knees, because my mother did not have enough fabric to make them long enough. No matter; I loved them anyway.

When I was in third grade, I was called into the vice principal's office. I had no idea why he called me; I was nervous. When I walked to the office, there were two older boys already standing there. I stood at the door and hesitated. I heard the vice principal ask, "Did your parents teach you to do it?" Both the boys replied at the same time, "No." The vice principal looked very serious. He saw me at the door. He said, "Come in. All of you are here. Do you know why three of you were sent to my office?" I shook my head and did not know why he asked that question. He said, "I am going to investigate what you three did yesterday after school." I still did not know what I had done wrong. He added, "Picking up stuff from school property is a serious problem." The other day while we were walking back home after a workday, we spotted a few fava beans left in the field that we had missed that afternoon when we harvested them. Two older boys in front of me saw the few beans first and ran to the field to pick them up. I followed the boys and looked at them. The vice principal questioned the two boys for only a few hours because they admitted that they were wrong, but I was not that lucky.

The next day, he called me back to his office again.

He asked the same question again and again, "Why did you pick up the fava beans and not admit the mistake?" He further interrogated me. "Did your mother teach you to do it?"

"No, my mother did not!" I told him. "I did not do anything wrong." I thought he would know that it was common knowledge gleaning leftover crops was not a crime. He looked mad and told me to go home to think about my behavior. His baffling message confused me. Why did I have to think? Didn't I tell him everything? I walked out of his office and thought I would have no more trouble, but the next day, he summoned me to the office again. I was shocked and scared. Why had he called me again? Didn't he get all the answers already? When I walked to his office and said, "Vice Principal, I am here," he seemed not to see me at all. I stood in front of him for a moment and tried to see his emotional expression. His face was long and dark. I stood there like I had needles on my feet but could not move. He slowly raised his head and said, "As a student of new China, you enjoy the free education, the food, and all the amenities provided by the communists. You need to have correct thoughts."

I lowered my head and said, "Yes."

He suddenly became very angry and spoke loudly, "Why don't you admit that you made a mistake?"

"Yes, I was wrong, but—" I did not have the nerve to continue what I wanted to say.

"Now you have admitted you were wrong. Today, I am going to teach you the correct thought."

"Yes." I lowered my face, watching my big toes scratching the hard dirt on the mud floor. I didn't say anything back to him. Tears dropped from my face and fell to my feet.

He kept saying something again and again about students in new China needing to have "a correct conscience." As I stood there crying, his stern voice sounded lower and softer. Suddenly, he said, "Now you know what correct thought is."

I shook my head and didn't reply.

"Be Chairman Mao's good student."

"Yes."

"Now you can go back to your class."

I ran back to my class. He spent three days harassing me, and I was quiet all the time except crying during the last day of interrogation. In order to save face, he just asked me to be Mao's good student and let me go. After that, whenever I saw the vice principal's face, I was frightened.

In my childhood, I learned that people going to the field to pick up the leftover crops was permittable. After the harvest in the village, the villagers who lacked grain for the year usually brought their chickens to the field to glean the leftover as feed.

Before we had the residency permit, my grandparents did not have enough grain to support the three of us. I used to help my grandmother to bring her chickens in two cages to the field after the harvest. She put the chickens in one place, and we scavenged the other place. At the end of the day, the chickens' stomachs were full, and they went back to their cages by themselves. We would also gather almost seven to eight pounds of leftover grain for the day. My grandmother would then carry the two cages of chickens with her wooden pole dangling on her shoulder, and I would help her carry the grain home. Whenever we went gleaning, my grandmother asked me if I was okay not having lunch. I told her I would be fine. I understood my grandmother's thinking because eating would take time away from gathering and getting the chickens back to the cage in the afternoon. From the experience of gleaning, I realized that doing so after the harvest was permitted. Therefore, I did not admit that I made a mistake during the vice principal's questioning.

On June First, International Children's Day, we were very excited because the school had different activities, like games and riddles. Anyone who won a contest or figured out a riddle could get candy or two litchi fruits. One booth was for guessing riddles; two teachers were there, including the vice principal. There were more than ten students there who tried to figure out the riddles. I squeezed in, and soon I figured out almost all the riddles, of course earning the candies. Other students glanced at my candy with a bit of jealousy, but they looked at me with admiration. In the end, the vice principal seemed to try to block me out of the game. He told me my answer was wrong, and he even analyzed the riddle with another teacher. I stood there with skepticism but did not dare to say a word. I was sure my answer was correct because the riddle was something like, "A squared material comes with news every day." I told him it was the newspaper, but he insisted it was a book. Luckily, another teacher, Mr. He, argued with the vice principal and asked him to check the answer. So he did, but he did not say anything; I stood in front of the two teachers like a log, wishing they would give me candy. Later, Mr. He gave the candy back to me. I got my candies and gave a few pieces to other students, and then walked away with a few classmates.

A teacher's influence can stay with a student for a lifetime. Some students grow up full of confidence because of their teachers. Some are always afraid because of their teachers. In my school, about one-third of the teachers were from the local villages; the rest of them were from different cities. Some of the local teachers were prejudiced against students who were from landlords' families or the so-called Five Black Categories. When I had the local village teachers, I feared going to school. When I had teachers from the city, I always felt secure and happy to go to school.

Those city teachers came to my school for different reasons; my teacher Ms. Yang was a college graduate. Some were the Red Guards who never finished school from the city, they were sent to the countryside by Mao's calls. In reality, Mao achieved his Cultural Revolution objectives by the Red Guards and wanted to dissolve the Red Guard's problems by sending them to the countryside. Some were from the Five Black Categories' families. They had been sent to the countryside to be re-educated by the peasants. All those teachers from the city were very friendly with my family regardless of their background. One time, I was surprised that they came to my home and discussed current affairs even though my mud house was the smallest in the village. They had no chairs to sit on, so they sat on our bed. Ms. Yang was very unhappy about being assigned to my school. She sometimes expressed her opinion on international politics, which was a strange thing for village people to understand. Most village people did not like her, especially the leaders. When the production team distributed fish to the villagers during the holiday, she did not get her share. She complained that she worked so hard but did not get any fish from the production team. My sister told my mother what had happened to Ms. Yang. My mother said that we needed to help her. Therefore, whenever the production caught fish on holidays, we went there to get her portion and bring it to her.

I also remember another teacher, Ms. Chen. She treated me like a living doll and loved to cut my hair whenever my hair grew long and tried to make it into different styles. Even though I was an elementary school student, I could feel her love for me by the tenderness of her eyes when she looked at me. A student like me who came from a family with a bad label longed for this kind of mercy for so long.

My junior high school math teacher, Ms. Qiu, was one of the Red Guards. She described her experience with pride and how excited she was about being a Red Guard in Tiananmen Square and seeing Chairman Mao. Mao smiled and waved to them; there were thousands of the youngsters like her gathered below. Mao's message to the Red Guards was to carry the torch of the Cultural Revolution to the far corners of China, to pursue the revolution to the very end. While she was describing the scene of greeting, she was full of joy and excitement, and her eyes were filled with tears. She told us that she also went to Mao's hometown to worship him. Every student looked at her with admiration; I could not help feeling jealous that she had been so many places, but I never expected to see our great Chairman Mao because of my family status.

However, her husband Mr. Fan was very quiet and serious. He was my sister's Chinese teacher and was very nice to her. He was also a Red Guard who didn't finish his school in teacher's college because the school closed for the revolution. He never mentioned anything about being a Red Guard. I heard stories about him from other people. He went to Tiananmen Square, too, to be greeted by Chairman Mao. On the way back from Tiananmen Square, he and other Red Guards saw an army truck passing by filled with soldiers. Those Red Guards robbed everything from the soldiers and hijacked the truck.

A few years later, the teachers had a conference. Mr. Fan was at the meeting. Coincidentally, the person who gave a speech in the meeting was a veteran soldier who was in that truck. He became a leader in the education department. While he was giving a speech, he immediately recognized the teacher who had hijacked his truck. The retired soldier called him behind the stage and questioned him as to what happened to the truck. No wonder Mr. Fan never showed off his pride in the revolution.

CHAPTER 16

MY FURRY FRIENDS

I ALWAYS LIKED ANIMALS, especially their babies. In my childhood, I had so many furry friends in my tiny house and small yard. My mother knew that I liked animals; she brought chicks and let me take care of them; she used to give me an allowance of about 0.01 yuan a week for learning materials or candy. Instead of buying candy for myself, I saved that money plus a little money from my sister to buy baby ducks. Whenever I saw those yellow fluffy baby ducks and chicks in the store, I just could not resist buying them, even though I knew I had to spend a lot of time and effort to take care of them.

By the time I was eight years old, I had twelve chickens, including one rooster. They were usually well behaved. They knew where they belonged and where they did not belong. One day when I came back from school, I saw a hen on top of our little mud house. The roof of the house was made of dry rice straw, hay grass, and bamboo. So there might have some grain left there. The hen looked very proud. She pecked a little bit, raised her neck high, and clucked. It seemed like she was saying, "Here I am. I am on the top of the roof, and here I have a lot of food." I sat on a chair and looked at her; she was so cute. Later, a rooster flew up there, and then all the other hens flew up there one by one. It was weird that the chickens flew. All of them pecked and pecked, but only the rooster raised his neck and crowed. I knew that it was not good for the chickens to peck the roof since my house was a mud hut.

It would be a big problem if they continued to peck, but I just couldn't get them to come down because they really enjoyed being up there.

Later, when my mother came back from work, she immediately made the chickens come down and yelled at me. "How could you just sit there and watch the chickens peck the roof without doing anything!" I didn't say anything and just walked away. How could she know that for me, watching the chickens peck the roof was enjoyable!

A few days later, there was torrential rain at night, and the house was leaking badly. There were water drops everywhere, even on top of my bed. We woke up during the night and used all the buckets and kitchen utensils to catch the dripping water. My mother even got a raincoat to put on top of our bed. That night I greatly regretted letting the chickens peck the roof. My mother spent more than a month of her salary to buy the materials to fix it. For many years, and even now, the chickens pecking the roof continues to be one of my most beautiful mental images. This picture is ingrained in my soul.

Chickens are like dogs or cats; they recognize our house and come back every night. All my chickens shared their food when I fed them, but whenever a neighbor's chickens came and wanted to eat, my chickens would not hesitate to chase them away. One time, when I came back home from school, I saw six of my chickens were missing. I called for them, "Gu gu gu!" but those six chickens didn't come back. I started to cry. My mother said: "They ran out and got lost. Don't cry. I will buy two chicks for you." In reality, my mother sold those chickens to the commune to count for the government's twenty pounds of meat per person contribution requirement quota.

Each person in the countryside was required to

contribute twenty pounds of meat to the government. The authority only allowed each family to raise a formulated amount of farm animals according to how many members were in the household. They had to sell the required amount of those animals to the government at the government's whole buying price and exchange for some meat coupons if the amount exceeded the required quota. If anyone raised more than the regulated amount, he or she would be considered going on by the "capitalist pathway" if they sold their animals/meat to the black market for a high price. (In the Great Famine around 1962, a pound of pork was twelve yuan per pound. In the early '70s, a pound of pork was about 3.9 yuan to 4.00 yuan per pound. It was much higher than buying it with coupons in the government stores.) If someone got caught, the product would be confiscated, and he/she would be accused of being a "capitalist roader" at a public accusations meeting.

I got two little ducklings. One died in a few days, and the one left behind was very sad and lonely. Luckily, my cat just had three babies, so I put the surviving duckling on the cat's bed. The cat did not mind the duckling walking around on her body with her kittens. She became a mother to the duckling. When the kittens followed their mother cat, the little duckling followed them. Later, when the weekly countryside market opened again, I begged my mother to buy a few more ducklings to accompany the one at home, so she bought four. They were so cute. I used to hold them on my lap or put them on my face to feel their downy feathers. Other people put their ducks in fenced enclosures, but I didn't. When I walked out, my little ducks followed. When they grew a little bigger, I brought them to the canal, and they were very excited. They swam around and dove into the water to find food.

Sometimes I put a leftover, small, salted fish head in the water; it was small as the size of a green pea. The fish oil expanded on top of the water, and tiny fish would come to try to eat the fish head and taste the oil on top. At that moment, my ducks chased the fish and ate them. I left them to play by themselves, and they knew when to come home in the evening. Whenever they were hungry, they came home for food. As some new feathers started to grow out, they grew up and acted like teenagers; they often disobeyed me. Despite the fact that I spent hours calling them back, they refused to come home. Instead, I saw them still swimming around the canal or the pond. Once I saw them, I would never forget to entertain myself. I dove into the water and poked them under their stomach. They were shocked and flew away. After they landed, and they looked back curiously to see who poked their stomach. When they saw me, they looked like I was still their owner or friend, and they would shake their heads at me and say, "Quack! Quack!" Then they went happily quacking down the canal. One day, the ducks disappeared; I spent the whole afternoon checking all over the ponds and the canal and tried to imitate their voice, "Quack! Quack!" I hoped that they would hear it and come out, but they vanished from my sight. I cried and missed them very much. I blamed myself for letting them run wild.

I didn't know if someone caught them for dinner or sold them on the black market because all villagers knew each other, so no one worried anyone would take your animals to eat or sell unless they ran around wild.

One time, I went to Big Uncle's house and saw my aunt-in-law bought a half-dozen goose eggs. She was trying to use her chicken to incubate the eggs. She put a brown chicken into a cage with the eggs. The goose eggs were about three times larger than the chicken eggs. The chicken looked at the giant monster eggs under her butt; her face turned red, her feathers puffed, her legs were shaking; she was so scared that she refused to sit on the eggs. My aunt-in-law tried to push the chicken down; once she removed her hand, the chicken immediately stood up and ran away. She then changed it to another hen; the hen saw the huge eggs and escaped as well. All her chickens treated the goose eggs like bombs. My aunt then tried a small bamboo cage just the size that could cover the hen on the nest and put a rock on top of the cage so she could not stand up. Unbelievably, the chicken butt still refused to touch the eggs. My aunt-in-law was very frustrated.

I said: "My Big Black can do it."

"Yes! Your old black chicken."

Later that day, my aunt-in-law came to my home with a basket of two dozen chicken eggs and said to my mother: "Your old big black chicken has seen the entire world. Can I borrow her to hatch my goose eggs?"

My mother replied: "Sure! You can try." Big Black laid eggs every day, but when chickens incubate eggs, they will not lay eggs. So my aunt-in-law gave us the eggs for compensation. I held Big Black and followed my aunt-in-law to her house. When I put Big Black in the cage, she saw the big eggs, and she made subtle sounds of pleasure and sat on them. After about twenty-seven days, the goose eggs hatched one by one. The lovely little goslings followed the black chicken as if she were their mother.

After that, I begged my mother to buy some goslings for me. We bought six goslings; they had olive-green and yellow feathers. I could not stop holding them because they were so lovely looking. In the beginning, I fed them with lettuce. Soon the goslings thought I was their mother;

they followed me all time. Geese grow fast; by the time they were three weeks old, I started to walk them next to the Pearl River to eat grass. The geese were very happy to go out. They waddled behind me like tough bodyguards. When strangers walked closer to me, the goslings would not hesitate to bite their legs. I felt so proud that I had all these guardian angels protecting me. One time, my cousin met me with my geese; she tried to catch one of them, but the geese escaped and faced her in attack position. I told her, "Just sit here. Look at me!" My cousin sat. I made a gesture and walked toward the geese. The geese just let me hold her. I then put the geese on my cousin's head and said, "Don't move." The geese sat on top of my cousin's head, then surprisingly poopooed on her hair. I broke out laughing. At the same time, I felt so sorry for her.

My geese were big and fat compared to other geese in the village because I took good care of them. My mother worried that someone might intentionally exchange my big fat geese with their skinny ones, so she cut a pinch of their feather on their head as the mark. That way, I would not lose them. At about seven weeks old, the goose's feathers grew like an adult's but the wings were still not strong enough to fly. One day, while they were eating grass, one of the goslings accidentally dropped into the river. She tried to come up, but the current was too fast that she could not stop flowing with the current. I was very nervous. I kept calling her. She replied, "Honk, honk" and tried to flap her wings, but her wings were not large enough. I wanted to jump into the river to carry her back to the shore, but my mother's tone rang in my ear, "Never go into the Pearl River! No matter what happens!" I chased the one in the river while five other goslings followed me. Once for a while, they looked down to check their sibling's situation in the water. They seemed to talk to each other with their honk, honk language. Later, all of them jumped into the water. That made me panic; I cried and said, "Come up! Come up! Please." First, they enjoyed the water for a few minutes, then they tried very hard to come up to the shore, but they could not make it. I was sure they understood I worried about them. I followed them for three to four miles; luckily, there was a small dam open to the canal. The goslings swam into the canal and came up one by one. On that day, it took me a few hours to get them home. My mother was very worried. At night, I got an idea to let the geese have full stomachs without going close to the river. The next day, I walked the goslings to our family's retained land since my mother planted many Chinese cabbages there. I left them alone and took out a picture book to read. I thought the gosling might eat the green outer part of the cabbages. When I finished my book, I found out all the cabbages had big holes in the middle; they ate the most tender heart part of the cabbage. I was so dumb that I did not think geese had long necks with their bill to choose the tender parts. The cabbage would not grow anymore. The geese were full; their food was swelling up to their necks. A few tucked their heads inside their wings; some stretched their legs, they all sat on the ground with a satisfying feeling of satiety. They were so funny looking, making my disappointment go away.

When I woke up the next morning, I found that all of my geese were gone. I was so sad and frustrated. My mother told me that I could not keep the geese because going to the river was dangerous for me. I cried and cried for hours.

My mother knew I loved animals so much, so she never slaughtered my animals except when my father's relatives visited us. Even though she had to, she did it while I was not at home because I always blocked my mother and told the chickens or ducks to run for their lives.

I had a beautiful female calico cat. She always looked aloof and acted elegantly. She had four white feet. Therefore, I named her Snow Feet. She had babies every year. Her babies were always reserved by neighbors and friends because she was the cat that really knew how to catch mice. People believed her babies must be as smart as their mother. Every time when she had babies, she refused to sleep on her bed and always carried her babies to my bed. Then I would put her babies back in her bed. She did not like it, and she kept carrying them back to my bed. We did that back and forth a few times. Later, since I had no choice, I put my clothing on her bed and made it more comfortable and prettier, so she stayed. Her meal was usually a small, salted fish head mixed with a half bowl of leftover rice. Sometimes I did not have any salted fish, so she only had white rice. She was very disappointed and looked at me and said, "Miao," and then walked away. She probably went to catch mice. She usually caught a whole family of mice: two big fat mice and four to five small ones for her babies to play with. One early morning, after I just woke up, I heard people talking loudly outside of my house. They said that my cat caught a big fish that was heavier than she was and wondered how she could even pull it up to the shore. One woman said the fish was at least three pounds, another one said it was at least four pounds. A man joined the gossip and spread his left hand to the right to show how long it was. The fish became bigger and bigger from their description, but they all felt that they were losers because they didn't get the fish before my cousin robbed it from my cat. I felt that was not fair since my cat spent so much energy catching it. By the time I saw her, her fur was wet, her tail was tucked instead of held high, and her ears were held back. She was definitely unhappy.

I loved animals so much, and they were all my buddies. When I was about nine years old, my mother decided to raise a pig in order to fulfill the yearly twenty pound contribution of meat per person required by the government. At that time, people used lard from the pig to make cooking oil since all peanut oil was exported to Hong Kong. To have oil, one must have coupons, but the coupons were only available for the city residents. So often we did not have any plant oil for cooking; our dishes used to have no added oil at all. People who lived in the countryside had to raise a pig or other farm animals and sell them to the state at a state-imposed price to get some meat coupons.

We built a pigpen next to the house. The pig was not easy to take care of. He yelled so much in the early morning before we woke up to bring food to him. My mother had to go to work, so my sister and I woke up before dawn and spent an hour making food for the pig. His food was sweet potato vines boiled with chopped trunks from banana trees and grain skin. When I brought the food for him, he walked quickly to his food trough and sniffed to see if it had anything good. Once in a while, I had leftovers from our dinner, like the salt fish sauce from my meal on his food. Then he gulped and sucked, making swishing and swooshing noises, anxious to get everything at once. Once he finished, he asked for more. If I had just the boiled plants without anything added, he just tasted a little bit, raised his head, looked at me, and said, "Oink. Oink. Oink." And then he walked to the corner of his pigpen. He looked very pitiful. I felt sad because I woke up so early and spent so much time making the food for him, but he refused to eat. I could not give my portion of rice to him because he ate a lot. He seemed hungry all the time, and of course, skinny. He did not sleep as much as other pigs; instead, he made a lot of noise, especially in the early morning. I felt sorry for him; then I let him come out from his pigpen, which made him very happy and quiet. He put his strong snout into the ground and began digging, pushing, and rooting. He loved to walk behind me, so people usually saw a pig following a little girl.

It took one and a half years to raise my pig to sell it because we did not have many food scraps for the pig to eat. At full maturity, my pig was around one-hundred fifty-four pounds. The government only accepted a pig that was more than one-hundred-fifty pounds.

One very early morning, I heard the pig screaming, and my mother was talking with my second uncle. Then I fell back to sleep until sunrise. I hadn't slept that long for a long time because my pig used to wake me up. After I woke up, I hurried to make food for my pig, but it was strangely quiet. I went to check the pigpen and found out the pig was gone. Suddenly, I felt something was missing from me, except for sadness and emptiness. Later in the morning, my mother came back, and she handheld two pounds of fat pork lard. I cried and said, "Where is the pig?"

"Look, we are going to have cooking oil!" she replied.

"I don't want oil. I want my pig."

My sister walked toward my mother with a smiley face. She asked, "Mama, did you sell the pig?"

"Yes."

"Yeah! We are going to have meat to eat today."

"No, I don't want pork. I want my pig," I replied.

My mother replied to both of us. She said, "I sold the pig, we are not going to have meat, but we are going to have lard."

We spent one and half years waking up in the early morning without enough sleep just to feed this pig. In the end, we could not have one bite of it. The disappointment and bitterness rose like bile into my sister's heart; tears fell like a waterfall. I always thought my sister was the toughest person in the world. She would not cry unless something was very wrong.

"Don't cry. Don't cry." I held my sister's hand, lowered my head, and cried, too.

My mother stopped talking and walked away. She knew that it was no use to explain to her children that each countryside resident was required to contribute twenty pounds of meat to the government each year. Our family had to meet the sixty pound requirement; my pig met two years' worth of that requirement.

As I grew older, I had a new member of the family, a black female dog. We named her "Ju," which meant Pearl in Chinese, like the Pearl River. Since we used to call her by saying "Ju Lai" ("Lai" means "come"), her name later became "Julai." Julai had lovely fluffy fur. She was very gentle, so my cat used to bully her.

All these animals were my friends, but not all humans were friends. There were some scary visitors. One day, after I came home from school, one local leader brought two strange men to look for my mother. I told them that my mother was at work or at my grandma's house; they walked away from me. Later, my mother came back from work and passed by my grandmother's home. My grandmother suddenly came out and asked her to get into the house. Once my mother walked into the house, there was a bowl of rice on the table that was already scooped. My grandmother asked her to eat it. My mother was hot, hungry, and thirsty; she ate up the rice in no time. My grandmother just stood next to her nervously watching, as if her daughter was eating the last tasty meal of her life. My grandmother made my mother eat because she was afraid that my mother would be too worried to eat at all after learning about the visitors. My mother sensed something was very seriously wrong. She asked her mother what had happened. My grandmother closed the door and took a breath, then said that two government investigators came looking for her. They wanted to know where my father was and to investigate my parents to see if they had any connection with Taiwan. My mother was shocked because, at that time, anyone connected to Taiwan had a bad ending and would most likely end up in jail. Indeed, my father had an old cousin who went to Taiwan with Kuomintang's army. My grandmother told them that my mother was clean and had no relationship with the "outsider." Before these two men left, they said that anyone who failed to draw a line between oneself and the traitors who chose to live abroad would be considered a "reactionary." My mother was constantly tense and worried that they might come back to question her. If it was not one worry, it was another.

CHAPTER 17

THE SEVEN ESCAPES

WHILE MY MOTHER CAME BACK to my home village in 1968, my father was on the run with his friend Wu Lin as fugitives trying to escape to Hong Kong. Before 1997, Hong Kong was still occupied by the British government. My father went to Huiyang, which was in the southern part of Guangdong, close to Shenzhen, about sixty-five kilometers away from Hong Kong. There, my father met an old friend, Mr. Hong Chen, from his hometown. Hong was from a rich family in old China. His grandfather was a county executive in the old government, and his father was a big landlord. During the Land Reform Movement, his father was executed, leaving behind his mother and five children. After the execution, his mother and his older brother went to pick up the body. The bloody scene caused the older brother to have a mental breakdown. He sometimes talked to himself and seemed extremely fearful of something. Unlike his brothers, Hong was a stronger boy, so he survived during the Great Famine. Unfortunately, his two siblings starved to death. To escape from the violence and humiliation, he left his family and became one of the vagrants in Huiyang, searching for freedom.

My father, Wu Lin, and Hong Chen stopped at Huiyang. First, they needed to find a job to survive. Because it was a border location where many local laborers had escaped to Hong Kong, there was a shortage of workers. But without the proper documents, they couldn't work there. As a result, they made fake documents indicating that they lived in the next county in order to apply for a job. Since they spoke Cantonese, the local officials believed them and hired them as tree cutters. They would work in the daytime, and after work, they needed to study *The Select Works of Mao Zedong* and express to the officials how it transformed them. They worked for a while and had little savings, but they feared that sooner or later, the officials would find out about their background. Thus, they were extremely alert, ready to run away if there were any signs against them. One day around 9:00 P.M., Hong Chan said that he wanted to go to the bathroom. He never came back. The militia could not find him, so they immediately gathered to form a search team.

Following a rush of footsteps, a man pointed in the direction of the bathroom. "He walked out just fifteen minutes ago. He must still be around."

"Hurry, we have to search in the woods in every direction. He is not too far away!" a leader ordered a group of men.

After searching for a while, a few men came back. My father did not see Hong Chan, and he sensed that there was something wrong. His heart was beating frantically; he hoped that Hong could get away, but also worried about his own situation. At about 10:30 P.M., one of the local leaders came and told my father secretly that the militia was going to have a big public accusation meeting the next morning, and my father was one of the targets. He told my father, "You must leave at two in the morning. At that time, there will be no one to spot you." My father did not want to leave by himself, so he told his friend Wu Lin the secret. In the silence of the night, they both disappeared into the deep forest. They ran as fast as they could in fear of the militia chasing after them. Their bodies were quaking and sweating. They stopped until there were no signs of anyone chasing them. After they left, they never had a chance to meet their benefactor again, the local leader who tipped off my father. In reality, not all the officials and militia were bad. Some of them sympathized with my father, and they knew my father didn't do anything wrong to the country. After leaving Huiyang, my father and Wu Lin started their journey to escape to Hong Kang.

Hong Kong is a peninsula. It has less than ten kilometers of land bordering mainland China, which is connected by a common mountain range and rivers. Today, the whole area bordering Hong Kong has become a major city, Shenzhen. In the '60s, Shenzhen was still a rural area. There were three layers of restriction lines near the border of Hong Kong. The restricted area spread from about nineteen kilometers deep and to ninety-one kilometers long. The first line was the borderline, the second line was the forbidden line, and the third one was the warning line. All three lines were under surveillance and guarded by soldiers, militia, and trained dogs. Only with a special permit could people access the border area. Anyone who entered this area without a permit was treated as a defector. If any escapee did not obey the warnings, the soldiers would fire a warning shot, and then they could shoot the person if they did not stop. Wutong Mountain is one of the restricted areas that many escapees had to go through, including my father. The mountain was located to the east of Shenzhen, facing Mirs Bay of the South China Sea. Countless escapees climbed over the mountain, but no one knew how many reached their destination. Many were caught by the soldiers or by the militia. Others died halfway across due to hunger. No one knew how many bones of fugitives had been left behind.

On the first attempt to escape to Hong Kong, while my father and Wu Lin were climbing over the Wutong Mountain, they heard a loud voice shouting "Stop!" just about a hundred feet away. My father immediately raised his hands. Wu Lin ignored the order and ran off. Within a second, my father saw a soldier pointing a gun at him. The soldier marched him to an army station, and from there, he was escorted back to Guangzhou City. My father feared going back. A background check would surely mark him, and then he would be sent back to the labor camp. A person from a family of "bad title" who attempted to escape only once would be sent to a labor camp for three years or more. However, a poor peasant who was caught for the first attempt of escaping would be sent to a re-education camp for a month or shorter. The government considered poor peasants the "teachable" citizens. My father was indeed sent back to the camp. Luckily, one day my father was able to run away from a job site because the guards at the labor camp were not well trained.

My father was on the run again. He walked aimlessly in a strange land and had no courage to go back to the place where he used to be. The hunger and misery gave him hallucinations; he dreamed that he was relaxing in a house with his wife and children around him. Thinking of his family was his only lifeline while living on the edge of survival. Therefore, he went to Zhongshan, close to Macau, where my mother, sister, and I were. He did not care what would happen to him; he just wanted to see his family. At that time, there was a slogan, "The counter-revolutionaries cannot escape the people's net of justice, even if they flee to the remotest parts." During that time, travel was controlled by the government, and anybody who visited friends or relatives had to have permission from the authorities and bring all the documents to the host's local police to register. Strangers who came to a village could be stopped by local security and asked to show their documents.

My father was able to make it to my maternal grandmother's village. But he was spotted by some patrol guards. A neighbor, Ah Po, the one who loved to tell old stories to the children across the canal, also saw him. She was trying to help my father hide by sending a boat over to pick him up while the guards searched for him. Despite these efforts, my father still could not get away from the guards, and he got caught. My father was not able to see my mother, my sister, and me.

When the guards arrested him, my second aunt just came by. She begged the guards: "Could you let him stay a little? I am going to call his wife to see him."

"No, he is an important fugitive, a counter-revolutionary. We got the order to send him back to the Guangzhou police immediately!" One guard replied.

Walking out of the village, my father turned his head and told my aunt: "If there is a good man around, ask your sister-in-law [my mother] to marry him and forget me in the future. She will be suffering if she continues to be my wife. As long as she raises our two daughters, I will be very happy even if I die. . . ." My aunt followed them a while and wiped her tears with her sleeves.

Later on, when my sister and I passed by my aunt's house, she was sitting next to a sand dune and making a basket with bamboo. When she saw us, she shook her head, then started weeping. I looked at her with curiosity; she told us what had happened to my father: "Your father was here earlier today." She paused. "The squads took him away." She paused again. "You two must behave and listen to your mother. . . ." I was not able to understand what she meant but felt something must be very wrong. My sister held my hand tightly, and my aunt cried uncontrollably. The mental picture of my aunt crying is still clear in my mind today.

Later, my grandmother talked about what had happened the day my father was taken away. The police station in Zhongshan ordered two armed militiamen to escort my father back to a labor camp in Guangzhou City because his census register was there. One of the two armed militiamen turned out to be my grandma's godson. My grandmother exhorted her godson not to harm my father and to take care of him on the way. He replied to her that he would, but only if my father was not going to run away because he would get into big trouble if my father escaped. By turning his gun on his own relative, he faced an internal clash between following orders or following his conscience. He knew that my father was struggling for survival and his freedom. Many years later, my father told me, "I did not want your grandmother's godson to get in any trouble, so I obeyed him. Otherwise, it was easy for me to break away since those two militiamen were holding broken rusty rifles." As a side note, when I was a child, I saw my grandmother's godson came to help my grandmother cook in different holiday celebrations. I heard that when he was born, his mother had a difficult labor and died. My grandmother saw the baby without a mother and felt pity, so she went to help and became the boy's godmother.

With all the bad labels placed upon my father by the authorities, it was no wonder that many of the countryside residents avoided his wife and children. The villagers asked my mother to go back to the city. They wanted us to leave not only because we were a family with a "bad element" title, but also because the three of us would share their grain and other coupons.

My father attempted to escape seven times. Whenever the people's militias or the soldiers caught him, they added years to his labor camp time. He knew that if he could not escape, he would have to stay in the labor camp or jail until he became a very old man or possibly for his whole life. Therefore, each day when he went out to work with other labor camp workers, he would plan his escape for his life, even risk facing death.

Years later, he told me his escape stories. "I always walked through the mountains at night and slept during the day. There were a lot of wild boars roaming the mountains. When boars see people, a big one will pose in a position to attack, and the others stand behind." Another time, he told me, "I was walking on the mountain at night, and I heard that militia were approaching. I quickly dropped down, but probably those militia heard some movement, and they walked to my hiding place less than a few feet away. I immediately rolled down into an open grave next to me. Luckily, some vines were holding me in the middle of the hole. The militia recognized the old grave; they didn't look down and walked away quickly because they feared ghosts!"

For another attempt, because walking across the border was almost impossible due to heavy security, my father had no choice but to swim across Mirs Bay, also known as Dapeng Bay, to reach Hong Kong. When he crossed over the Wuntong mountain and reached the bay, he discovered that the tide current was flowing in the opposite direction of his destination. He waited anxiously but was filled with confidence that he could get to Hong Kong this time. A soldier came by and was only two feet away from him, so my father held his breath and hid between the bushes like a rock. While this soldier was walking back toward the station, another soldier came out with a guard dog, "Woof! Woof!" The dog pounced on my father. The result was the same, adding a few more years in the labor camp.

In the labor camp, there was a lake where the detainees washed. My father would swim in the lake every day, but someone reported to the authorities that my father practiced swimming to improve his swimming skills because he wanted to escape to Hong Kong. To defend himself, my father recited Mao's quotation: "Promote physical strength and build up the people's health." The person who accused him could not say anything in reply because Mao was the "god" that no one could challenge. My father learned that using Mao's quotations was his best defense.

The last time my father failed to escape, he almost got killed. When they caught him, they questioned him. "Where did you come from?" Since he had a record of escaping from the labor camp multiple times, he could not tell them the truth. He also could not tell them that he came from Guangzhou City or Zhongshan since his name was on the blacklists in those places. Instead, he told the soldiers: "I came from a poor peasant family in Gaozhou," which was his hometown. He said "poor peasant" because they would not punish a poor peasant badly. Mao considered "the poor peasants" as the base for the communist party. When poor peasants did something wrong, they were only required to do some Mao study, then be released. Unfortunately, this time they escorted my father back to his hometown, which was far away in the western part of the Guangdong province. The militia escorted him onto a train with their guns. My father realized he was facing a serious problem if he went back to his hometown since his family background was a landlord, not a poor peasant. Besides, he had also joined the Youth of Three Principles Organization when he was in high school. With all of these, he would be charged with the serious "counter-revolutionary" title. They would not send him back to the labor camp; instead, they would send him to jail, which was a much worse place than the labor camp. Before the train arrived at the Gaozhou station, he hit upon a way out of the predicament. At great risk of his life, he jumped off the train while the train was moving fast. The militia did not have the nerve to jump, so my father was able to get away from them.

My father seriously injured his leg. His leg was in pain. Fearing that anybody might recognize him, he did not go anywhere to buy food. He had a home where his mother was always waiting for him, but he could not go back. If he did, the militia would be waiting for him. Prolonged hardship and deprivation were eroding his mental and physical powers in a frightening way; he was too tired and too hurt to move. He was plunged into despair. Fortunately, his youngest cousin, who was called "Little Brother" by the family, lived close to where he had jumped, so he dragged himself with his injured leg to his cousin's home. His cousin did not recognize him because my father was extremely thin and pale. It was clear that my father had been out of food for days. "It's me, Little Brother." My father's voice was very weak.

Little Brother was very shocked; he brought my father into the house immediately. He wanted to treat my father, but he was flustered. Although his cousin had inherited some of his father's medical skills, his medical knowledge was very limited because he had only a little education. In his area, children born of a family of a landlord could not go beyond elementary school. Therefore, he immediately called a real doctor, who was his father's friend, to come in secretly to check on my father's leg. Once the doctor saw my father, he was in shock.

"How could he make it to the house with this kind of injury? It must be extremely painful!"

"I don't know. When I opened my door, he was lying next to the doorstep. I could hardly recognize him."

"You need to help me to adjust his joint. One of his joints tore and twisted a little bit."

The doctor injected a few acupuncture needles to numb my father's leg. Then he asked Little Brother to restrain part of my father's body. A "crack" sounded, and my father almost screamed aloud, but then he felt much better. The doctor stood up and exhorted Little Brother to take good care of my father.

Before he left, he talked to my father. "Son, you will be fine. Your uncle talked about you when he was alive. He was always proud of you. We all miss him." He walked out of the door and turned back to my father and said, "Feel peace of mind and convalesce here. I will be back within three days."

"Thank you very much, Doctor!"

My father soon recovered, having stayed there for almost a month, then told his cousin that he had to leave.

"You cannot leave. Your leg is not totally recovered yet."

"I cannot stay here for long. You will get into big trouble if someone finds out."

"It is okay. No one will find out you are here."

"I don't want your life to be ruined. Besides, my leg is fine right now."

Little Brother took out all his savings—fifteen yuan—and gave them to my father. My father left his cousin to search for his freedom again. He walked slightly differently after the incident. After his leg was injured, he was in despair and had almost no courage to live on. He felt that his prospects were bleak. In his eyes, he was on a vast sea without a boat, unable to spot an island in sight. He had never had that kind of hopelessness, even when he was in jail.

My father's escape journeys became mostly solo adventures. Other than one layer of clothes, my father carried nothing. When evening fell, he hiked on the empty mountain. As nights wore on, a deathly silence filled the valley. Without a watch, he had to look at the stars at night to see what the day of the month and the time of the day it was. He learned how to find water to drink in the wilderness. Years later, he told me: "When you see different kinds of trees around, then there is water close to you. If you see only the evergreen trees, then there is no water." Sometimes there were clusters of blue flames that flashed in the silent night, suddenly bright and then dark again, which gave haunted fear to the escapees. They called them "ghost fires." When my father walked closer to look at them, he saw a pile of bones. The bones were from dead animals or humans, perhaps escapees. My father knew the flames were phosphorescence from bones, and he was not scared at all. In the earlier escape attempts, other escapees liked to follow him because of his knowledge and survival skills. However, my father learned that if a group of people tried to escape to Hong Kong, once caught by the government, the leader of the team received capital punishment. At that time, three or more people were considered a group. Therefore, he avoided going with others. He said there were some advantages and disadvantages. The advantage was he did not feel bored—at least there was somebody to talk to. The disadvantage was they drew attention, so the soldiers and militia spotted them easily. To avoid attention, he chose to go solo.

In one of his escape attempts, he was extremely hungry. He had been hiding for a long time with no food. He saw some tiny snails on the ground, the kind that had a long cone shell growing in the swamp area in the tropical and subtropical areas. They can cause serious diseases: blood fluke parasites, lung fluke parasites, and Hepatitis B. Despite the dangers, my father picked them up and used a rock to break the shells and ate them. Growing up, we were told those snails are not edible due to bad bacteria. My father not only ate them but also picked up extra snails and put them into his pocket for his next meal. Since my father had escaped a few times already, he knew that there were too many army stations located closer to the Hong Kong border. He was able to cross the station while the soldiers were changing shifts. One time, after crossing the army station, he reached the bay. However, the soldiers caught him after he was about a hundred feet away from the water. The soldiers who caught him kept saying something smelled so bad, not realizing there were rotten snails in my father's pockets. At the army station, all the soldiers covered up their noses. "Smells horrible! Where did you catch this stinky man?" "Woof, woof." An army dog pounced on my father. A soldier called the dog away, searched my father, and found two pockets full of rotten snails in his short trousers.

Each failure made my father try another seashore

farther away from Hong Kong for the next attempt. Being farther away also meant that the bay was closer to the open sea. People who tried to swim to Hong Kong in the open sea over a long distance typically could not survive in the water, so it was a less guarded area. During a night in the summer of 1970, he made his final attempt to escape to Hong Kong. When he started to get into the water, he saw so many fireflies. He looked at them and thought they were a symbol of hope, a good omen. He suddenly felt that he would be able to get to Hong Kong this time because the fireflies represented the light at the end of the tunnel, and they also matched his name, "Rong," meaning the glory of light. While he was swimming, he saw some other escapees getting into the water and swimming toward Hong Kong. Unfortunately, one by one, they disappeared into the dark open sea.

My father was an excellent swimmer; his skill helped him to swim continuously for seven to eight hours that night. He ate anything that he bumped into: jellyfish, seaweed, and any other small fish. He had no more fear. After a while, he forgot about the sharks and the hunger, and he swam and swam. He was lucky that sharks did not eat him; there were so many escapees who died of shark attacks. When he reached Hong Kong, it was early in the morning. He was very excited to reach his goal, but he also had an upsurge of emotions. He had survived, but he left his whole family in mainland China: his mother, his wife, and two children. He reached Hong Kong when I was about six years old, and we still didn't know if he was dead or alive.

Chapter 18

ARRIVAL IN HONG KONG

WHEN MY FATHER REACHED the seashore of Hong Kong, he only possessed a pair of shorts he wore, a five yuan bill, and a three-pound food coupon. The bill and coupon were the lifelines that he had kept as a last resort. He had managed to hold on to them for almost two years. When they were vagrants, my mother had pulled out a tiny cloth bag from her pants and put this bill and food coupon into it. She stitched this bag to my father's shorts and urged him not to use them unless it was absolutely necessary to save his life.

After the long swim, my father looked like a green monster because algae covered his body. He landed on the coast of Hong Kong close to a barn. Hungry and exhausted, he used his last bit of energy to walk to the barn, hoping to find something to eat. In the barn, there were many pigs but no pig food left. He collapsed and fell asleep. He did not know how long he had slept.

"Mister, wake up! Wake up!" A man's voice brought him back to the world. My father slowly opened his eyes and saw an old gentleman who was trying to rouse him from lethargy. The man was a farmer who had brought the food to feed the pigs and spotted him.

"What happened to you?"

"I just swam here from Mainland China."

"I know. I have seen many escapees," the man said, and he brought my father to his home and offered him a meal with rice and a salted fish. That meal was absolutely delicious for my father; it was like the best meal he had ever had in his whole life. He would never forget that meal and the kindness of that old man.

While my father was eating, the man said, "Do you have any relatives or friends in Hong Kong?"

"I have a few old friends in Hong Kong," my father told him and provided the farmer with their names.

The man tried to find the names in a phone book, but there was no match.

My father said, "I know a friend, Hong Chen's uncle, is a professor of a university in Hong Kong. I only know his name, but I don't know which university exactly."

"I know a way to find the professor's address if you are sure he will accept you," the man said.

My father was not sure of the professor's current situation, but he had heard his friend Hong Chen speak about his uncle while they were cutting trees in Huiyang about a year before. The man said, "The British Coast Guards would stop in a certain area at a particular time. They can find the professor for you." He hesitated a bit but continued, "If the professor won't accept you, and you can't find anyone else to accept you, then you will be sent back to China by the British authorities."

He offered to bring my father to the coast guard. My father took a risk and agreed. The man took him to the British Coast Guard after he rested for a while. Before the man pointed to the boat of the British Coast Guard, he warned my father, "You'd better think twice before going there. If they cannot find the professor, the British government will send you back to China!" My father did not reply. The man lowered his head and said, "You seem to have no other choice. I tried my best. Good luck!"

On the boat, there were already other escapees. A

coast guard ordered the escapees to go below deck. He warned them that the Chinese militia might stop the British boat at any time and search for the escapees. The British sailors could not do anything because the British government needed the Chinese militia to block the escapees fleeing into the Hong Kong colony.

From the beginning of communist rule in China to the end of the Cultural Revolution, the British government treated the escapees differently at different times in response to social issues in China. When the British government could not handle that many people were fleeing into Hong Kong, the colony tightened its policy on allowing the escapees to enter. During the Great Famine around 1960 and the Cultural Revolution from 1966 to 1976, thousands of Chinese people swamped in every day. As a result, the colony tightened its policy by sending the escapees back to China. Even though the government did not want to keep the escapees, the local people suggested the colony should let them have a full stomach before sending them back because these escapees were severely lacked nutrition due to famine in the mainland. Within a short time, tons of money from nonprofit organizations and the rich donated money. Once the escapees entered Hong Kong, the colony fed them a good meal and then sent them back by train.

When the time my father got to Hong Kong in the summer of 1970, the British authority allowed escapees who reached Hong Kong to stay only if they could be vouched for by relatives or friends in Hong Kong. While it is true that many escapees died on the journey to Hong Kong, those who successfully crossed the border were again chased and arrested by the police in Hong Kong.

I heard many stories of how the escapees accidentally

jumped off the Eagle Mouth cliff, also called Tiger Mouth cliff, on the Wutong Mountain close to Hong Kong at night. Many escapees died there because they walked at nighttime on the mountain; suddenly, they saw the lights not far away from them. The dazzling city lights of Hong Kong made the escapees over-excited, and they ran ahead to their dream place. Unfortunately, they ran off the top of the cliff. Some of them went another route; they walked through the water pipe before the pipe started to run water from China to Hong Kong since China supplied the fresh water to Hong Kong.

The British colony feared being swamped by Chinese escapees, so the escapees were not welcome. However, for humanitarian reasons, every day, the British government sent out boats to save the people who were still alive in the water and to pick up the dead bodies along the coast. Those escapees who were not found by the government snuck into the city and tried to blend into society.

Typically, escapees were classified as refugees by the international community. Because there was no international aid to help alleviate the economic burden, the British government did not welcome Chinese escapees even though the local people sympathized with them because they were also Chinese.

My father stayed in a detention house for a few days in Hong Kong. British officials offered him milk and bread in the morning. A social worker helped him find the address of the professor, and two social workers even accompanied my father to visit him. When they got to the professor's house, he was not at home, but his wife was. Since she was a local resident, and her husband had never mentioned my father, she did not know my father.

At first, she did not open her door for him, and my

father was very nervous; his legs were shaking and his heart was pounding because he was worried the British would send him back to China if no one vouched for him. He explained, "Aunty, I am from your husband's hometown, and your husband's youngest brother Ah Wang shared a house with my family in Guangzhou City. I am also a friend of your husband's nephew, Hong Chen." She was skeptical, so she picked up the phone and called Hong Chen. She asked some questions. My father was very worried she would hang up the phone. My father said, "Can I talk to Ah Hong?" The woman gave the phone to my father. When he picked up the phone, he cried out, "Ah Hong, I am Rong. I am in Hong Kong at your uncle's home right now. Please help me!" Hong Chen immediately told my father not to worry. He asked my father to give the phone to his aunt. Hong Chen, who we now call Uncle Hong, had escaped to Hong Kong three months earlier than my father, and he was working while my father talked to him. He explained to his aunt that my father was his best friend and begged her to let him in the house. She invited my father into her house, thanked the social workers for their service, and gave them two hundred Hong Kong dollars, which was equivalent to thirty-three US dollars in 1970. A social worker comforted my father before she left. She said, "Mr. Chen, you don't have to worry about being deported back to China now. You will be fine." My father was relieved.

When the professor came back home from work, he was happy to see that my father had arrived in Hong Kong safely, but he also had so many mixed feelings. He told my father that his younger brother Ah Wang capsized in the sea while he was trying to escape to Hong Kong. He let out a sigh and inexpressible sorrow for his brother's death. My father was shocked to hear the news, and his mind could not stop the appearance of Ah Wang's image for days.

The professor's wife took out a few pieces of clothing and told my father to wear them. The professor told my father to stay at his home and to share a room with Hong Chen. His wife saw my father had severely swollen legs, so she made a remedy out of a few pounds of garlic boiled with some other ingredients. He drank it for a few days till his swollen legs went back to a healthy size. My father always appreciated the kindness of the professor's family.

After passing the hurdle of entry, my father knew that finding a job had to be his first priority. As such, he accepted any kind of offer. His first job was to carry coffins up to the mountain to bury the dead. He worked long hours, but he was happy that he could earn money and send it to his mother, his wife, his sister-in-law, and others. He knew that money was not only important for the family but also provided emotional comfort. At the very least, his family knew he was alive and working in Hong Kong. He did not know how he had so much energy to work. He and his co-workers worked long hours. By the time he walked down the mountain, it was already late in the evening.

People who lived on the mountain slope talked to my father. They asked, "How come you work up there until the evening? Aren't you scared of the ghosts?"

My father replied by joking, "I want to catch a ghost. I can ask the ghost what the lottery numbers are for the next day, so I will not have to work so hard."

CHAPTER 19

THE "SPY GIRL"

WITHOUT A FATHER, I was an easy target for bullying by others in the village. My mother, a single mother, could not protect me. A woman raising her children without a husband was subjected to ridicule and gossip by the neighbors in the countryside. Consequently, her children were victims of the ridicule. Worse than that that I was called a "bad element's daughter" because people knew that my father was arrested and sent to the labor camp. On top of all these reasons, I looked weaker than other children due to malnutrition. My posture was not good at all; some people even gave me a nickname, "Three Curves" because my back was hunched, my belly pointed forward, and my legs curved back. That was caused by a lack of nutrition and calcium. Worst of all, I stuttered when I got nervous. All of these disadvantages magnified the perception of my ineptitude. The others knew I would not fight back if they bullied me.

In my childhood, I felt my maternal grandmother was the most important for me because she always protected me and offered me the best. I always felt so comfortable with her. There were no words to describe the relaxed feeling with Grandma. In contrast, I feared my mother because she always seemed to have a heavy heart laden with anxiety. No matter how I was bullied by others or suffered from humiliation by teachers, I did not go home to complain and tell my mother what had happened to me because my mother always turned her back on me and said in a low voice, "You are not well behaved." I did not get any comfort from her; instead, I got punishment for misbehaving. I learned the lesson that no matter how innocent I was, I had to put up with everything. At home as well as in school, my sister was the only one who always understood my feelings and protected me if anyone bullied me.

Although the Chinese government forbade citizens from going to Hong Kong, there were still postal connections flowing between the places. Many people in Hong Kong supported their relatives living in mainland China by sending money. There were chances of risk for the relatives with "foreign connections" to be accused of being a foreign spy depending on what their status was in China. While my father was in Hong Kong, my mother never mentioned anything about him to me. However, one time, my mother asked my sister and me to write letters to my father when we had just learned to read and write in school. My first reaction was, "Where is my father?" For a long time, I had already accepted that I did not have a father. Indeed, I did not have any memory of him. But my mother still did not tell me where he was. I told her, "I don't know how to write a letter. I am only in the first grade." My mother said, "Just copy what you learned in school." So for my first letter to my father, I copied one of the lessons in my Chinese book: "Long live to Chairman Mao!" and "Good health for Vice Chairman Lin!"

My family received little support from my father during his early years of living in Hong Kong. He did not send us very much because he also sent money to his mother, his older brother's family, his sisters, his aunt, and all of his cousins, leaving almost nothing for himself. My mother understood him and knew her husband's personality. All she wanted was her husband's devotion. A letter from my father was like a light in the darkness that illuminated her heart, giving her the courage to live on.

After my father went to Hong Kong, some villagers called me "a spy's daughter." I had no idea why they called me a spy's daughter because my mother and my sister never told me my father was in Hong Kong. When I walked alone by myself, a group of kids often yelled at me, "Spy girl!" and threw clay at me. I was so scared when I saw those kids, and I ran away as fast as I could. The fact was I could avoid them sometimes, but not all the time. Once my mother asked me to buy a cup of soy sauce for her, and I had to walk to a state-owned store about three miles away from my house. While I was walking, a few of the children hid behind the corner of their houses and yelled, "Spy's daughter! Spy girl!" Suddenly, clay flew over my head and fell like torrential rain all over me. I ran but fell and crashed hard to the ground. I felt dizzy and passed out for a few seconds. I tried to get up, but I saw stars flying around me. I cried loudly and went back home with a big bump on my forehead. My mother looked at me and asked what had happened. I told her the whole story. She was sad but didn't say anything. From that day on, I was scared to walk alone to the store. I had an instinctive sense of tension while I was passing by that area. I knew those children had collected a pile of clay, and they were waiting to insult me.

One of the bullies was my cousin, Tian; he was a short but sturdy boy. When he talked, his eyes would slant on one side. He liked to say nasty things to other people. He always targeted kids younger or weaker than him, such as girls like me, but sometimes he was not that lucky; some of the kids would beat him badly. He liked to target me because his mother instigated him out of jealousy of my maternal grandmother, who took care of me better than her children. Tian would find any chance to beat me up. One day, I went out to pick up burning leaves for cooking. He stopped me and claimed the leaves belonged to him and then took them away from me. I said: "No, they are mine!" Then he punched me furiously with his fists. I ran away from him as fast as I could. He yelled to my back, "Catch the spy girl!" As a result, on that day, I had no fire leaves to bring back. I told my sister what happened. Fortunately, my mother used to save some fire leaves in the corner of the stove, so my sister and I were able to cook.

One day my mother went to town in the summer of the flood season, all the dams were closed to prevent flooding into the canal. The villagers had no fresh water to drink since when the water in the canal was not flowing at all; we called it "dead water." It meant not drinkable. Everybody in the village had to carry water from outside the levee in order to cook. My sister and I brought a big bucket. We went to the river to get the water and carried it home with a hardwood pole. I walked in front, holding the pole on my shoulder; my sister was in the back. The water bucket vibrated between us. On the way home, we stopped under a longan tree to rest. Suddenly, Tian came with his older sister and claimed our bucket of water belonged to him, then started to carry it away.

"Stop, it is mine!" my sister said.

"Say it again?" Tian replied, and he added, "Ah Jade may just want to experience my fist."

"I dare you!" my sister said.

Seeing them arguing with each other, I was very nervous, and my heart was pounding. At the same time, I was very proud of my sister for having the nerve to face him.

Tian immediately pulled off a few small tree branches with all the leaves on them. He used it to beat my face as hard as he could. Suddenly, I felt thousands of needles pointed at my face. I touched my face and the blood showed on my hands. I cried loudly without resisting because I could never fight back due to my weak body. While I was crying, Tian was proudly showing off how strong he was. My sister picked up the pole that we used to carry the water and beat on his back as hard as she could. Tian collapsed on the ground and started to cry loudly; his older sister dragged him up, and he walked to his nearby home. Soon, his parents came holding a pole. His father ran to us and yelled: "I am going to kill both of you!" Some villagers were carrying water on the same road, which was the only road that gets to the levee, and witnessed everything. One of the strong men immediately pulled his pole from his hands and said, "Kids fight. Adults should not get involved." A few of the adults came to stop them, too. One told them: "It was your son's fault. He beat Ah Jade first." My sister finally cried out; she seemed to cry out all her grievances. She was my hero. After that, my sister became famous as a tough girl in the village. Some kids would not bully me anymore when I was with my sister.

But it was not only kids who mistreated me. One day, I argued with a classmate before the class started because that student called me a "spy's daughter." The teacher walked in, made me stand up in class, and asked why I argued with the other student. I stood up, looked at that student, and said, "He called me a spy's daughter." The teacher replied with a weird smile, "If you are not a spy's daughter then who else would be?" He humiliated me in front of the whole class. I was so angry and speechless and felt the entire world could not accept me. I tried hard to hold onto myself, by my tears fell uncontrollably. It was strange that I could forgive that student within a few days, but the teacher's nasty face was stuck in my mind for a long time.

Many years later, I asked my mother why she always blamed us when other people bullied my sister and me. She said that if we could survive at that time, then we were already very lucky. She told us that if she hit us then hopefully other people would make less trouble for her family. She added, "I hit you once, and my heart ached once. You did not know how difficult it was." She then became reticent for a while.

Now I have children of my own, and I could not imagine that if others bullied my children, I would not protect my children but punish them instead.

CHAPTER 20

PATERNAL GRANDMOTHER'S LAST WISH

LETTERS KEPT COMING from my paternal grandmother from Gaozhou. She desperately wanted to see my sister and me. She wrote that her health was deteriorating from day to day. She knew that she would not have any more chances to see her son again in her lifetime but wanted to see her grandchildren before she died. She requested my mother bring us to Gaozhou. Every time my mother received the letters, her mind filled with uneasiness and worry because going to another town required an official approval document from the local authority. She had never told the village leader that her husband's hometown was a countryside village in Gaozhou. They thought my father was from Guangzhou City. When he was sent to the labor camp, he lost his city residence status, and my mother had to go back to her home village. As a married woman, her resident permit should align with her husband's, which was why initially the village leader didn't want to give us a resident permit. My mother discussed this matter with Big Uncle and my grandmother.

"What should I do?" my mother asked.

Big Uncle answered: "If you go, you need the approval document from our local authority. If they find out you hid your family's secret, they will accuse you of lying to the authorities, and you will get in big trouble."

My mother replied, "My mother-in-law treated the children and me very well. She was the one who took care of the children while I was working in Guangzhou City."

My grandmother advised her daughter with trepidation, "If our villager leaders find that out, they will cancel the resident permits for you and your children, and they will ask all of you to move out of here." My grandmother continued, "Once our commune cancels your resident status, Gaozhou will not accept you because your husband hasn't lived there for years. Besides, the title of your mother-in-law is a landlord."

My uncle added, "You will become homeless again if both communes don't accept you."

My mother was tired from the anxiety of worrying during the day and spending all night with her eyes shut, her restless mind unable to settle. Her mother-in-law's face flashed in her mind, working and smiling, as happy and contented as a grandmother could possibly be. Her love for the children was extraordinary. They had helped each other while my father was in the labor camp. Her mother-in-law was her refuge during the insanity of life's storms. But now she could not even send her children to see her. My mother's heart broke and she said, "I will never forgive myself if my mother-in-law dies without seeing my children."

We did not go to see my paternal grandma in Gaozhou, and she got more worried. She heard a rumor that a single mother left her children in our village to get remarried. To make sure that was not my mother, she sent her youngest daughter Guijuan to visit us. Auntie Guijuan was married to a man in the border area near Macao. She brought all her four children to our house, two girls and two boys. Her children were younger than I. They seemed to have never seen the outside world before because they were nervous and very shy whenever they saw a stranger. Guijuan complained about her miserable marriage and poor living conditions. My mother comforted her and said, "I am your older brother's wife, so please treat me as your mother. Come over any time, whenever you need to." She persuaded my mother to visit my grandmother. My mother explained to her the dilemma she was facing. Guijuan understood and said, "I will explain that to my mom."

My aunt stayed for two weeks since making the trip was not easy for her. She lived near the border of Macao, which is a restricted area. My mother borrowed some money and gave it to my aunt. In addition, my mother used all the fabric that my father had sent from Hong Kong to make shirts for her two little boys. She also made a cloth baby carrier for her, which was a traditional thing for a mother to make for a daughter who had a baby. She knitted a beautiful flower pattern and stitched it onto the back of the carrier. Hopefully, Aunt Guijuan's husband would not look down on her and let her come over again.

My mother did not have enough material to make shirts for the two older girls. On the day they were supposed to leave, the two girls were reluctant to go and looked at their brothers' new shirts. My mother summoned my sister and me and said, "The two of you, take off your shirts; I am going to use them as samples to make new clothes for you." My sister and I were thrilled and took off our shirts. My mother took them and immediately handed them to my cousins. When we realized what was going on, our clothes were already put on their small bodies. I looked at my mother and mumbled but did not have the nerve to say, "How could you do this to me? That is my favorite clothing." Tears of despondency cascaded down my cheeks. I looked at them walking away, and I did not miss them, but I did miss my clothing. My sister was very unhappy, too. She pulled my hand and told me not to cry.

After Guijuan left, my older cousin Yinsheng came from Gaozhou. He was sent by my grandmother Nai Nai, and he told my mother that my grandmother really wanted to see the kids before she died.

My cousin said in a blaming tone: "How could you not bring your children to see her? Every morning when Grandmother opens her eyes, she wants to see her grandchildren."

"If we go, we could lose our residence permit and not be able to come back."

"Well, if you see Grandmother cry, you would not say that. Grandmother Nai Nai said that she would not have any chance to see her son again, but she wants to see her grandchildren."

The next day, my mother did not care what would happen to her, so she went to the local authority's office to apply for travel permission to visit her mother-in-law. The officer asked some questions about Guangzhou and Gaozhou, and why my mother never mentioned my father's hometown. My mother told them that my father always lived in Guangzhou City after he graduated from school. The local leader said that he needed to send all the documents to the upper authority to review for approval. While my mother was waiting for permission, she received a telegraph from Gaozhou in the early summer of 1976. It said that my grandmother had died and asked my mother to bring the children to pay last respects. My mother rushed to the production team's office and asked if her permission had been approved or not. The leader said "no," and he suggested my mother go to the brigade office.

My mother finally got the travel permission. I saw her holding the consent form and talking to herself,

"Mother-in-law, I am sorry. It is too late...."

"When are we leaving?" my sister asked with swelled eyes. I saw them packing some clothing and some local products like dried vegetables into a small bag. I had no idea what they were doing since my mother did not tell me what had happened.

"Mama, where are you going?" I looked at them with curiosity.

"Your paternal grandmother Nai Nai died!" my mother told us.

I did not have any memory of my paternal grandmother because she left us when I was a baby. Therefore, I felt neither panic nor sadness. On the other hand, my mother felt the biggest regret in her heart that she could not bring us to see her mother-in-law earlier. She went to Gaozhou with my sister and left me at home with Po Po.

After my mother left without me, I had a weird feeling that I never had before. I wanted to cry for my paternal grandma but could not. I was so sad and felt as if a knife was piercing my heart. As of today, I still cannot explain why I had that feeling.

CHAPTER 21

THE CAMPAIGN TO DESTROY THE "FOUR OLDS"

THE CAMPAIGN TO DESTROY the "Four Olds" was one of the initiatives of the Cultural Revolution. (See Appendix A-8.) The Four Olds referred to old ideas, old culture, old customs, and old habits. Mao mobilized the young people to destroy the Four Olds because the Four Olds interfered with the creation of the new socialist society. Every day we heard the loudspeaker from the production team broadcasts, "If we do not eliminate the roots, the plant will grow back. We must eradicate these relics of the past." In the beginning, I thought the Four Olds meant old, used objects.

When I was a young child, my best evening activity was to go to my Big Uncle's house to listen to his storytelling. Every evening, there were at least a dozen kids and teenagers gathered in Big Uncle's front yard, some sat on the ground, and some sat on chairs. Big Uncle sat on a big "executive" wooden chair, which was made by his oldest son, and put a small table next to him with a teapot. Since there was a shortage of real tea, his tea was made from the leaves of the longan tree. Big Uncle's stories were from some famous Chinese classical novels such as *Journey to the West* and *The Romance of the Three Kingdoms*. One time he was telling an episode of how the monkey king fought with the ox beast, when all of a sudden he stopped. He sipped his tea and said, "If you want to know the next, come back tomorrow."

I said, "Big Uncle, continue! What happens next?"

Then all the kids yelled, "Continue! Continue the story!"

In reality, Big Uncle had forgotten the story. He took out the book and started to read it. One of my cousins at the door ran to him and said with a low voice: "The security guys are coming!" During the Cultural Revolution, the neighborhood security guard or the Red Guards used to go door-to-door to check the residences. Especially in our area close to the border, they claimed that "they need to look at the foreign spies hiding in the village." So they looked for any strangers in the household. They also wanted to crack down on any Four Olds activities. My uncle immediately hid his classical novels under his chair.

The guards showed up. One of the guards asked: "What are you all doing here? Anyone see any anti-revolution activity?"

Everybody in the yard was quiet and scared.

Big Uncle took out Mao's small red book and said, "We are studying Mao's quotes."

"Really?" the guard couldn't believe Big Uncle would volunteer to study Mao's book. Big Uncle started to read some lines in the red book: "We must have faith in the masses, and we must have faith in the Party. These are two cardinal principles. If we doubt these principles, we shall accomplish nothing...."

One of the old customs identified for destruction were traditional wedding ceremonies. One day in early 1976, I was walking back from school. As I entered my village, an old lady I called Auntie Liang saw me and told me with great urgency, "Go, run! Tell your second aunt that some people are coming!"

I had no idea what she was talking about. I hesitated a bit, but a lady pointed to a group of people less than a mile away from us. I followed where her finger pointed and saw five to six young men and women walking to our village.

The old lady yelled, "Hurry! Go, run!"

I stared blankly at her and thought, *Why?*

"Just tell your second aunt that some people are coming."

I ran as fast as I could. Once I stepped into my aunt's courtyard, I saw a few tables and benches were placed there. There were about twenty people who were busily preparing food for a secret wedding for my cousin. Some of them cut fresh vegetables and meat on top of the tables. There were lotus, cabbages, gingers, scallions . . . Others were cleaning fish. There were few chickens in a cage under a table. My second aunt was placing some incense in a vase on top of a tall bench in front of an ancestor's plaques.

I was out of breath and told them, "Some people are coming behind me."

The second aunt asked me, "Who is coming?"

I answered, "I do not know, but Auntie Liang sent me here to tell you."

Once they heard that, they acted extremely fast; some people moved the table back inside. Some people hid the food; some people took down the incense, ancestor's plaques, and the god's altar from the bench. In my hometown's tradition, people put an ancestor's altar in the living room, and they also built the god's altar with the statue of Buddha on the wall of the front entrance. But during the Cultural Revolution, they removed the statue of Buddha. Other people took down the incense from the top of the kitchen range. People believed that a kitchen god was always helping to watch over the fire, so they also put incense on top of the kitchen range. Some people took the food through the back door of my aunt's house and walked away. The bride almost burst into tears. At that critical moment, my uncle sent her and a few other people to walk to my house from the back of my aunt's house. Of course, I walked back to my home with the bride.

Once I got inside my house, I looked out of the window and saw that a group of people was swaggering with insolence toward my aunt's courtyard. When I looked closely, I recognized them. They were all the young Red Guards from the city. The bride burst out crying when she saw that group of people walking to her new home; my mother kept saying quietly, "It's okay. It's okay. Don't cry." About a half hour later, the Red Guards walked out to the street with hostility, full of anger.

As soon as the Red Guards left, we walked back to my aunt's house with the bride. The second aunt was still filled with great fear. She said, "They stormed in my house and also invaded the bride's new bedroom."

"It is okay. Our children will be fine," the second uncle replied.

My cousin, the groom, sat on a chair like a log. He seemed worried about something. In my hometown, only the groom could enter the bride's room during the official wedding day. It was very insulting, rude, and bad luck if people got into the bride's bedroom before the groom. The Red Guards came and tried to find any of the Four Olds like the practicing of worshipping ancestors and god on the wedding day. However, they could not find any sign of worshipping gods or the ancestors, but they smelled the incense and the food. They were furious and questioned my aunt and said that they saw a little girl ran to the village and that girl must have alerted her before they walked in. My aunt and other relatives just simply told them, "No." The Red Guards had heard about the wedding, and they thought they could find some evidence of the villagers still practicing the old customs, but they got nothing. When they left, everybody was relieved. I became a hero of the family.

The next day, my second uncle and aunt invited many people to their home for their son's "official" wedding. What happened was that my aunt planned two wedding ceremonies, one was the real traditional wedding, and the other ceremony was the one to show the village leadership the new Cultural Revolution-style wedding. During the Cultural Revolution, people in my hometown used to hold a secret wedding in the traditional style a day before the open celebration, so they could follow the three traditional procedures in order to become a husband and wife. First, they lit the incense in front of the ancestor's altar in the living room and the god's altar on the outside entrance of the house. Then the new couple first prostrated themselves to heaven and earth, and then they had to prostrate themselves to the parents and their ancestors. Finally, they prostrated to each other. After the three procedures, they would be officially married. They then walked to their new room.

When I walked into her home the next day for the open ceremony, it was a very different kind of environment. There was no incense at all, not a sign of the old customs. A few village leaders and some brigade cadres came to celebrate. They put a picture of Mao in front of the living room, and the new couple bowed to his picture and promised that they would be loyal to him. After they bowed to Mao's picture, everybody was happy and clapped their hands. I felt it was fun to watch them kowtowing.

During that time period, practicing religion was considered Four Olds and was prohibited. But people still worshipped god and their ancestors secretly on the traditional holidays and other special days like weddings and funerals. I often saw people lighting incense outside their houses. I was sure that they lit incense inside the houses as well. My mother sometimes lit incense during the first day and the fifteenth day of the month, which were the first day of the lunar month and the date of the full moon. Many people in the countryside did this early in the morning before dawn because they did not want any activists to see them. If someone was spotted by the activists or secretly reported by other neighbors, the village leaders and the activists would then plot a series of criticizing and denouncing public meetings.

Besides traditional wedding ceremonies and religious practices, Confucius' teaching was another one of the Four Olds that was prohibited. When I learned to read, books obsessed me. If I had a chance to read a book, I had to finish it before going out to play. During the Cultural Revolution, it was hard for people to get an interesting book to read because most books became forbidden. There was a "Criticize Lin and Criticize Confucius" campaign, and the schools distributed a few chapters of Confucius' teachings to be criticized. I found them very interesting, so I read all of them within a day. I heard my mother say that the people of China had been studying Confucius' teaching for more than two thousand years. Aa Pao, the older woman who lived across the canal who talked loudly, told us that when children went to school in the old days, the children had to prostrate to the picture of Confucius before the class started. I always believed my mother was right even though she was so strict with me, but sometimes I was confused about what the teacher taught us in school. In schools, the teachers unconvincingly portrayed Confucianism as an evil and reactionary ideology. At home, I continued to study Confucius' teaching. The Red Guards destroyed the artifacts of our ancestors' creations, but that did not mean they could destroy the old culture, the inherited values, and the beliefs. They could only eradicate the pieces of artifacts.

As Confucius's teaching was passed down in writing, all books written in the past were targeted in the Destroy the Four Olds campaign. One time, one of my aunts told me that my grandmother's attic had a lot of books of classic literature like *A Dream of Red Mansions, Journey to the West, The Romance of the Three Kingdoms*, and *The Water Margin*. I went up there and turned the attic upside down, but I could not find a single book. I was very disappointed, and I sat on top of the roof beam with two legs hanging down. My grandmother walked into her house and saw the two legs. She was shocked that I climbed so high and sat on a beam. I called out, "Grandmother!" My grandmother was relieved.

She asked, "Why are you up there?"

"I am looking for books."

"No more books. All the books have gone."

"Where are they?"

"All the books have been burned."

"What?"

She did not give me an answer. Instead, she asked me to come down. Her response was depressing.

Some families still had some books left from the old generation. Their children sold their books by weight in exchange for other necessities. The adults did not stop it, because in those days you could easily be called a bad element by reading books that were considered Four Olds. I heard a story of an old man who read a book about acupuncture in Chinese medicine. When he was reading that book, he tried to remember each acupuncture point. He wrote those points in his notes and tried to remember them. The Red Guards raided his house and found all those weird names. Since they did not understand acupuncture, they accused him of using those names as the code for spying activities. Allegedly, the poor man was beaten badly by the Red Guards. No wonder my grandmother did not answer my questions about why she burned the books.

CHAPTER 22

PUBLIC ACCUSATION MEETINGS

DURING THE CULTURAL REVOLUTION (1966–1976) in China, there were frequent "Public Criticizing and Denouncement" meetings. This type of meeting was a new version of Public Accusation meetings that originated from the earlier Land Reform movement. These meetings were meant to criticize, humiliate, and physically abuse people who were accused of not following Mao's socialist agenda, and they provoked hatred and violence among people. The worst example of this happened when some activists formed their own "people's court" to persecute "class enemies" and imprison people without proper legal process.

In our village, typical activists pulled some Five Black Categories people (landlords, rich peasants, counter-revolutionaries, bad elements, and right-wingers) onto the stage and beat, kicked, and interrogated them in public. All the villagers were required to attend. These events were very popular. Audiences ranged from a few hundred to a few thousand. The purpose of these meetings was to "educate the citizens to have class-consciousness and class standing against the class enemies." After the meeting, people were afraid to do anything against the rules. They gave up their humanity and blindly obeyed the power of fear.

When I was very young, I usually saw a group of people, typically the Red Guards, parading in the street. They escorted a few "bad element" people by tightening them with rope and putting dunce caps on their heads. The hat described each person as a "landlord," "counter-revolutionary," "spy," etc. One or two Red Guards held a loudspeaker, shouting, "Down with imperialism! Down with the landlords." The crowd then echoed these cries. Every time I heard the loud noise, I ran out to the street to look. I felt a little curious and baffled with horror at the same time. This was a typical scene after a public denouncing meeting.

One day in 1974, after morning school, it was drizzling. I was walking back home next to the canal. I saw a crowd looking at something. When I got closer, I saw a man lying in a small boat on a dock at the canal. His body was covered with a clear plastic raincoat; his bare feet curled on one side, and he was shaking badly. His face was ashen, and he looked like he was in extreme pain. I recognized him. The village people nicknamed him "Wheels" because he was a truck driver in the former Kuomintang army before the communists took over China. Obviously, he had been labeled a "counter-revolutionary" and was frequently tortured in the public criticizing and denouncing meetings. The sight of him scared me badly; I hid behind my sister; she tried to use an umbrella to shield my view and pulled me out from the crowd.

I heard people gossip: "He drank some DDT to commit suicide!" one woman said, and she added, "They wanted to pull him out again for the public denouncing meetings."

Another woman added, "They found out that he had poisoned himself when they came to interrogate him. . . ."

DDT, dichloro-diphenyl-trichloroethane, was a popular insecticide used in China in the '60s and '70s. It is a strong poison to humans and animals. A few young men rushed to the boat with paddles in their hands; they wanted to paddle him to the hospital. He died that afternoon on the way to the hospital. I knew he was a quiet man and never harmed anyone. After we came home, my sister told our mother what had happened. It seemed my mother already knew what the story was about; she was not surprised but warned us not to join the criticizing meeting.

"But sometimes our school requires us to go, then what can we do?" my sister asked.

"Never join the crowd and beat the landlords." My mother did not explain why; her expression indicated that it was an order. "Never boo with an audience. You are a model for your sister. Okay?"

Indeed, my sister was a model for me. I had no idea what she thought about the accusation meeting, but for me, whatever my mother told us, she gave us no alternative. For the next few days, when I went to school passing the same place where Wheels had lain, the image of his body shivering badly in the boat still came to my mind.

I started to get used to joining these kinds of meetings after I entered school. The procedure of the meetings was almost always the same. First, a leader stood on a stage with high spirit. He took out a little red book and read loudly: "Our Great Chairman Mao teaches us: A revolution is not a dinner party or writing an essay or painting a picture or doing embroidery; it cannot be so refined, so leisurely and gentle. . . . A revolution is an insurrection, an act of violence by which one class overthrows another." Then a few activists pulled out a few landlords and "bad elements." The leader started to announce the allegations against each of the bad elements and warned that the landlords always tried to sabotage the new society. As I looked around the meeting site, some of the audience joined the booing. Some of them were just spectators; their expressions reflected numbness. I was numb mixed with fear when the meetings became more violent. At first, I thought the landlords were the bad people because that was what I learned from the school and the propaganda picture books. I knew two of my aunts-in-law were from landlord families, but I didn't know my father's family was landlord, too.

There was a big public accusation meeting held at the commune level with seven production teams there. The site was in a litchi orchard with a temporary stage built there; on top of the stage, a slogan was written in a piece of white fabric and spread on both sides of the poles. The slogan was LENIENCY FOR CONFESSION, SEVERITY FOR RESISTANCE! A loudspeaker hung on a tree. Our school class was canceled, and we were brought to attend the meeting at the site. However, it was different this time; a group of people walked around the orchard; they were surrounding some litchi trees and booing. When we walked to one of the trees, there was an old woman landlord tied on a tree with a rope. One side of the rope tied her hands on her back; the other side was attached to the tree. She looked like a dog tied on a tree. There was a sign hung on her neck with the words: LANDLORD and her name. Her back was bent sixty to seventy degrees; her hair was a mess. Some kids threw dirt at her. Her eyes showed extreme fear that beat correspondingly in my heart. In the movies and the picture books, the landlords' wife was mean, cruel, greedy, but what I saw in front of me looked innocent and very pitiful. I felt sorry for her even though she was supposed to be a "blood-sucking landlord's wife." I never had any intention to join others in insulting the landlords because my mother and grandmother taught me not to disrespect anybody regardless of who they were.

Then my classmate pulled at my clothing and asked me to follow other classmates to see another landlord. There were a dozen landlords and bad elements displayed in that orchard. Each of them was tied to a litchi tree. There were a few teenage kids around those landlords; they poked at them and threw clay at the victims for fun. The adults watched them quietly, but no one prevented the kids' actions. My cousin Tian was one of the teenage kids. He took a small wooden hammer he made and used it to hit a landlord and made a silly face to the crowds. I ran away as fast as I could because I was afraid of him.

In the evening, Tian cried loudly, passing by my house; his father held a small bamboo branch, beating him badly. While he was beating his son, he said, "I told you never beat the landlords. Do you hear me?" Tian was like a nervous monkey; he warded off the bamboo branch by jumping around his daddy. He tried to run away, but his father held his arm and continued to beat him. I was so happy Tian had the punishment he deserved; he had bullied me so many times. Later I understood that Tian's mother was from a landlord family, and Ruen's mother was also from a landlord family. During the Land Reform time, they were forced to give away all their dowry like rings and gold to the government because those things were from their families, the landlords' families. The leaders in the village told them that after they married, they had to listen to the lower peasants and draw a clear line away from their landlords' families.

At night, Ruen walked into the neighborhood and sang a water song that he composed: "Tian went to beat the landlord to show his fealty. . . . When his father beat him, he wailed like a ghost and howled like a wolf, aow,

aow aow. . . ." By the next day, Ruen's song became popular in the village; all the kids sang it.

In the spring of 1976, I was in my first year of junior high school. One day, my teacher Ms. Yang came in and announced that we would not have a class that day. Instead, we would attend a meeting. I was quite happy about not having class. We followed our teacher to the meeting location. Once I got there, I could not believe my eyes. My oldest uncle, I called him Big Uncle, was on the stage with a rope tying his hands behind his back. His body was almost bent eighty degrees, a tag with a few words on it—I AM GUILTY—hung on his neck. I was very shocked. How could he be up there? He was not a landlord. I had so many questions. I had attended these kinds of meetings so many times, but they did not really bother me because they were not my relatives. This time, it really struck me. My classmates all looked at me and started to gossip. I felt so ashamed that my beloved uncle was up there, but my teacher Ms. Yang immediately stopped the students. I could feel that she was trying to protect me because she was always nice to me before I became an official student in school. Big Uncle and other "bad elements" wore big heavy winter clothes on that warm spring day, while everybody else around the stage wore shorts and T-shirts. Soon the meeting started. First, a leader of the village recited Mao's quotation; he said, "After the enemies with guns have been wiped out, there will still be enemies without guns; they are bound to struggle desperately against us, and we must never regard these enemies lightly." Then the leader announced the allegations against each of the "bad elements" on the stage; the accusations were a mixture of fakery, misrepresentation, and exaggeration. Big Uncle was accused of engaging in "capitalist merchant trading with speculation and profiteering" because he got caught for selling products in the black market.

In reality, my Big Uncle only raised a few farm animals and grew some produce, then sold them privately to others. At that time, doing business was considered "going the capitalist road." Every family in the countryside could only raise a limited number of animals according to their household registration. If anyone raised more than the set amount, they had to sell the animals to the state. Otherwise, it was considered to be "going with capitalism." Although selling farm products in the black market was not allowed, many bold people did it anyway. Local authorities mostly targeted the ones that had a different line of thinking or might have personal conflicts with the local leaders. I used to see my Big Uncle carrying a basket that hid some meat that he bought with the money he earned from selling his products. When I ran to him, he used to smile and secretly showed me the hidden meat. In those years, meat was very limited, and meat distribution was controlled by the government. Eating meat was even considered a capitalist sin.

Some of the men on the stage were accused of practicing the old culture, and, of course, some were landlords. The cadres always added the landlords to the list in the meetings. They were the unluckiest people at that time.

When the meeting started, the activists were excited, and they started to beat, kick, and pull the accused people's hair. One of the activists who beat the victims most was a young Red Guard named Liu from the city. He could not be a teacher like others from the city because he was not capable, but he did not want to do a farmer's work, either, because he was lazy. He liked to show off as a revolutionary activist. Liu jumped up and down on the stage repeatedly with a twisted face; he rolled up his sleeves and pulled my Big Uncle's hair back to make his face slant upward. He accused my uncle, "You have no remorse for going the capitalist route!" Then, he pushed my uncle's head face down onto the floor and kicked him and punched him again and again. At that moment, I understood why Big Uncle wore a heavy coat because the coat could protect him from the kicking and beating. While they were beating him, my heartbeat followed the rhythm of each pounding. My head felt swelling, and my blood ran fast in my veins. I lowered my head and closed my eyes to escape the scene on the stage. My classmates pulled my clothing from time to time and said, "Ah Jade, look at Liu. He beat your uncle again." I wished that it was only a bad dream, and it would end soon, but the scene was cruel reality. I looked at the meeting site; most of the audience seemed numb; they showed no sympathy and no compassion. One could tell they were brainwashed. When the meeting reached a high intensity, the organizer led the attendees in shouting, "Down with capitalism! Down with imperialism! Down with the landlords! Down with the counter-revolutionist! Down with the bad elements!" The crowd around the stage echoed the words. At the end of the meeting, a leader concluded the stage, said, "We should not be softhearted toward class enemies. We must strike terror into the enemy's hearts. Our meeting ended with satisfaction."

After the meeting, I walked back home by myself; my heart still fluttering with fear. Suddenly, my grandmother stopped in front of me and asked, "Did you join the denouncing meeting?"

"Yes, I did."

She immediately asked me if Big Uncle was beaten or not.

I told her the truth and also told her who beat him the most.

She continued to ask me, "Did your Big Uncle bleed or not?"

I told her no and also reassured her that Big Uncle wore a big heavy coat. My grandmother lowered her head and walked away quietly, but one of my older cousins walked toward me and asked me what grandmother asked me. I told her what I told my grandmother. She yelled, "How could you tell Grandma that? She is going to worry." She turned away from me and talked to herself, "Liu is not going to have a good ending!"

That evening, I heard my cousin, the son of my Big Uncle, vowing, "I am going to kill Liu if he goes back to the city in the future." The hatred between people was instigated during the Cultural Revolution.

Every time the village had a meeting, the activists always rang the bell in the village and announced the start of the public criticizing and denouncing meeting with a loudspeaker. One time, I walked into my grandmother's house and saw my mother and my aunt talking quietly. It was a rainy and chilly day. My aunt said, "A poor landlord wet his pants when he heard the village bell ring. When is their miserable life going to end?" My mother saw me, and she immediately made a gesture to my aunt to stop talking.

When the cousin sent by my paternal grandmother came to see us, he also got into big trouble in our village. At one of the public accusation meetings, I saw my ninth aunt and my cousin placed on the stage. Their hands were tied behind them, and they stood on stage emotionless like the other four young "bad elements" on the stage.

I saw some cadres interrogating them: "Are you trying to escape to Hong Kong?"

"This is treason!"

Fortunately, this meeting was not as bad as the typical ones because the activists didn't hit them very much. Everybody knew that in our village, escaping to Hong Kong was a young person's goal. Therefore, no one wanted to beat each other. Later I asked my ninth aunt why she was targeted on stage at the meeting. She said she had gotten into trouble simply because my visiting cousin was excited and jumped into the Pearl River behind our house to swim in the evening. The local people used to swim only in the canal instead of the Pearl River. Therefore, some people assumed that he was trying to improve his swimming skills to escape to Hong Kong. My aunt was just in the wrong place at the wrong time. She advised my cousin to swim with extra caution in the dangerous river, but the village activists reported that my aunt had tried to help my cousin to escape to Hong Kong. The next day after the meeting, when I went back to school, my best friend, who was one year older than I, asked, "What do you plan to do in the future?"

"I don't know," I said.

"I am planning to join the communist party or escape to Hong Kong," she told me quietly.

"Are you crazy? These two ideas go in totally different directions," I said.

"Do you want to have a good life? Good clothing?"

"Of course," I replied without hesitation.

I could not believe she could tell me that. She said that the reason she told me was that my father was in America. We became very close friends. I felt I was not a daughter of bad elements anymore. I trusted her very much, and she came to my home a lot. My mother always welcomed her.

There was another form of those public meetings called "Recalling Past Suffering and Thinking Over the Source of Present Happiness." At these meetings, there were usually a few poor peasants to give speeches. Their speeches were always on how they suffered in the old society, which was referred to as "before liberation," and how the landlords cruelly exploited them. They warned the students that the landlords tried to sabotage socialism and lead people back to the misery and suffering of the old days. They told their tales tearfully, then recalled how the new society turned their lives around. Mao was great, and communism was great. In addition, there were "taste the old society" events in all the schools.

One time, the vice principal of my school asked the students to find wild vegetables or weeds and bring them to the school the next day. He also required each student to bring a bowl. He said that we all needed to taste how the poor people suffered in the old society. The next day, I cut some sweet potato vines. Some students brought banana trunks, and some cut banana leaves; others simply cut grass from the wild. We gave all the wild vegetables to the school kitchen. The school's cook was an older man we called Uncle Qi, and he used to prepare food only for the teachers. When he saw so many wild vegetables piled up in front of his kitchen, he did not know what to do. We all stepped in to help. Some helped to clean the wild vegetables, and some scooped water from the canal. Uncle Qi kept picking out the grasses that were not edible. He let out a sigh and taught us which grass was edible, which one was not. But the vice principal put some weed back to add the taste of bitterness. We put all the wild vegetables and water into three big woks and stirred some bran into the mixture. A few students helped to make a fire. An hour later, all of the vegetable-bran mixture was cooked.

Soon the school bell rang, and the vice principal announced that we had an assembly of the "Recalling Past Suffering Meeting." In the meeting, a brigade leader named Jian-Fei from a neighboring village was invited to give a speech about his family's suffering before the Liberation. He talked with emotion when he said his brother and sister died of hunger. He cried loudly in front of the audience. In between the speeches, the vice principal stood up and raised his right arm and called out some slogans like "Down with the old society! Down with the landlords!" and all the students stood up and echoed after him. Some of the students were affected by the tears of the speaker, so they jumped to their feet, waved their fists, and vowed to protect the new society. On the other hand, the children of former landlords felt full of guilt.

The next person to testify was "Old Liang," who was one of the production team leaders. At that time, some poor, uneducated peasants were chosen to be the leaders. Old Liang was one of them. A few days before, he came back from a small town nearby where he had bought some ice pops for his grandsons. When he arrived in our village, he parked his bicycle where a few of us were playing around. "Hello, Uncle Liang!" we greeted him. He wanted to show us the ice pops he had bought, but only saw a few sticks in the small basket on his bicycle.

He said: "Hey! Some kids must have stolen my ice pop bars and, after they ate them, put the sticks back into my basket! What kind of joke is this!"

We looked at each other and made silly faces. A boy

stood up and said, "No one stole your ice pop bars. Don't you know that ice melts?" We burst out laughing, and when he stood up to talk, some of the students started to laugh again.

Then a teacher led the students to sing a song. The lyrics of the song were "The twinkling stars hang in the sky, and the crescent moon shines. The production team holds a meeting, complains of the grievances, the extremely old evil society. . . ." To this day, I still know how to hum the song.

I do not remember the rest of the brigade leader's speech. All I remember was that after the speech and the singing, we formed a line to go to the kitchen and were required to eat the wild vegetable-bran mix. We were told this was the food the poor people ate in the old society, so we had to taste how bitter life was "before the liberation."

Each student held their bowls in line in front of the kitchen. Uncle Qi and a few helpers scooped the watery, green, mashed wild vegetable-bran mix into the bowls. Some students laughed; some stick out their tongues into the green mash with a skeptical face. I scooped a spoon of the green mash put it into my mouth; the taste was weird: tart, bitter, astringent, and sour. The vice principal stared at the students and said: "You have finished all the food in your bowl." Since there were around four hundred students in the school, Uncle Qi and a few helpers kept adding the wild vegetables in the woks and made sure all students had the chance to taste it.

After the tasting, we were required to write an essay about how miserable the old life "before liberation" was and how sweetly we were raised in the new society. In the essay, we also had to express hatred of the landlords and be vigilant of the landlords.

The next day, I found out some students had stomachaches, but luckily I was fine. I asked my grandma: "Are these wild vegetables the food people ate before liberation?" My grandma just said: "I don't know." I did not get an answer from my grandmother, so I went to ask my mother. She replied, "Nonsense!" Of course, I would not tell others what my mother had told me.

I also heard some old ladies gossiping about the brigade leader "Jian-Fei's story was fabricated. I know his family history. His brother and sister didn't die!"

"It is a shame that he uses his tears to get promoted to the brigade leader position!"

After a few repeated meetings, we were bored with these kinds of meetings and hated to write the essays.

CHAPTER 23

CAPRICIOUS FATE

DESPITE LIVING IN VERY DIFFERENT PLACES, 1970 was a turning point for my father. He was able to escape to Hong Kong in the summer, and my mother received her residence permit in the countryside in 1971. They both got out of their most dangerous situations.

My father was alone in Hong Kong and could not see his family. He wrote to my mother and expressed how much he thought of her, and how he suffered from not knowing how his children were doing. He sent money and asked her to send a picture of his daughters so he could see how much his children had grown. He worked very hard during the day. But after a long day of work, only the emptiness and quietness waited for him when he came back to his room. The only way he could cope with the loneliness was to hang his family's pictures in every corner of his room. He collected pictures of his family members from all different places: pictures of my grandmother in Gaozhou; a picture of his younger brother from Guangzhou; a picture of my mother, my sister, and I from Zhongshan; and his own picture in Hong Kong. He took all those pictures to the photography shop and merged them into one picture with the whole family. He sent copies to my mother, my grandmother, and my uncle. It comforted my mother that she was always in her husband's mind.

Close to New Year's Day, my mother received some fabric and peanut oil sent by my father from Hong Kong. She made new clothing for my sister. Later, I wore the hand-me-downs from my sister. Even at that time, my mother still refused to tell me about my father, but I started to realize my father did exist. Once in a while, an image of my father emerged in my head. Occasionally I wanted to know his side of the family, his past, and of course, what he was currently doing. Sometimes I heard somebody gossip that my father had a car and drove everywhere in Hong Kong. For me, a car seemed like something that only the great Chairman Mao could sit in. I did not care what other people gossiped about my father. I just went my own way and did my own things. But often I thought if my family could have just a bicycle, it would be great!

One day, my mother took me to the county fair to look for vegetable seeds and other items. As we walked out to the street, a shiny car stopped in front of us. My mother's face suddenly shone, her eyes blazed like a torch. A man who said he came from Hong Kong got out and asked my mother if she knew someone in this area. My mother told him no. Then he got back to his car and left. My mother watched the car speeding away, her bright eyes turned mournful, and her shiny face immediately became pale. Later, my mother talked to herself, "Why not him? When is he going to pick me up?" I did not know the "him" in my mother's words meant my father. She dreamed that one day her husband would drive a car in front of her house and pick up her; then she would be very proud and would show the village people that she was not an abandoned wife.

After my father arrived in Hong Kong, the professor's wife helped my father and her husband's nephew Hong rent two rooms in her relative's apartment building, named the Five Alliance Building. My father was a very open and friendly person; soon, he became friends with everyone on his floor, so they knew these two men escaped from China and worked very hard.

One day in 1972, one of the neighbors, Mrs. Kang, had two relatives visiting her from the United States. Everyone called Mrs. Kang "Aunt Seven" because she was the seventh child in her family. She saw my father passing by, and she invited him into her apartment. She started to introduce my father to her relatives, Mrs. Ng and her daughter. Mrs. Ng immigrated to the US around 1949. She had a restaurant business in New York City. Aunt Seven told Mrs. Ng that my father was an outstanding man and worked very hard: "He is a good son! Good son! What a pity that he is not able to see his family." My father started to chat with Mrs. Ng, and they both talked very congenially. Soon they seemed like long-time friends, talking about their families and children.

Suddenly, Aunt Seven interrupted them and asked Mrs. Ng to petition for my father to go to the United States. She said, "You should do something for him. Otherwise, he will not have a chance to see his family again. Since he is still a refugee in Hong Kong, he cannot go back to China. If he goes to the United States and becomes a US citizen, then he can go back to China to meet his family." Life is full of unpredictable opportunities. Mrs. Ng was a stranger and had only met my father once, but she decided to petition for my father. Later, she also petitioned for my father's friend Hong Chen. She was a woman with a good heart and an abundance of compassion. She always helped people who had difficulties in their lives. We later came to call her "Aunt Two" because she had an older sister.

At the beginning of 1974, my father received a notice from the United States immigration office informing him that he was granted an immigration visa to go to the United States. At first, my father hesitated; he felt comfortable in Hong Kong. By that time, my father had become a contractor, and he just got a big contract to build an apartment building that was more than twenty floors. He did not want to leave his unfinished job. After he ignored two notices, the US immigration office sent him a final notice with a deadline of ten days to respond. Whenever he had to make a big decision, my father thought about his family first. Also, he knew that Hong Kong was going to be taken over by China in the future, a big uncertainty for those living in Hong Kong at the time. Ultimately he made the final decision to go to the United States. He subcontracted his job to his best friend, Wu Lin, who had changed his last name to Chen when he was a vagrant in China, hiding from the authorities. My father hastily packed up a few things before he headed to the United States on March 1, 1974. A photo of him at the airport surrounded by his friends shows the mix of anxiety and excitement as he prepared to leave. All his friends went there to say goodbye to him.

After my father came to the United States, he immediately wrote a letter to my mother that he immigrated to America; in the letter, he explained to her that this would give our family a chance to reunite after he became a US citizen, because at the time the Chinese government only allowed the Chinese people who were the immediate relatives of a foreign citizen to leave China. He worked in a restaurant owned by Mrs. Ng's husband, and soon they became good friends. They spent a lot of time together after they finished work at the restaurant. One day my father went to Mrs. Ng's home and took out a picture from his wallet and showed it to Mrs. Ng. He asked her which one of his two daughters she liked more. She looked at the picture and told him that she liked both, but the younger one looked sweeter than the older one. "The older one is going to go to high school next year," he said, "and the school is far away from home, so she needs to walk almost two hours to get there."

Mrs. Ng responded, "You should send a little more money to her so she could buy a bicycle and ride it to school. You need to take care of your immediate family first instead of sending a big portion to your nephew." In the old Chinese tradition, my father was supposed to support his brother's son after the death of his brother—especially since he did not have a son himself at that time. Mrs. Ng knew that, and she added, "Your wife's life is not easy. She is raising two girls by herself, but your nephew has grown up already. You don't have to take care of him." After that, my father entrusted his friend, Uncle Hong's wife in Hong Kong, to send many household goods to us like fabric, peanut oil, and pain-relieving aromatic oils.

Chapter 24

A LITTLE CAPITALIST TRADER

Our living situation improved a few years after my father went to Hong Kong. With the money sent by my father plus the diligence and thrift of my mother, we knocked down our small mud hut and built a small brick house in the summer of 1976. We were very happy that we did not have to worry about rainy days anymore. Also, my mother bought a bicycle. I did not have to beg my cousin to let me ride on his family's bicycle anymore. Our whole family loved the bicycle so much! On weekdays, my sister proudly rode it to school every day. I was about eleven years old, and my legs were too short to ride. I would wait for the pedal to come up, then I pushed the pedal down again and waited for the next pedal.

My mother also brought a transistor radio; we were one of a few families that had a radio in our village. Each day, there were a dozen people who came into my house just to listen to different information because everybody was tired of the loudspeaker announcements about the local production team's victory and politics. Sometimes when we were not at home they would use a bamboo pole with a hook to get our radio out via the window. Often, a dozen of people sat under a longan tree next to my house; they sat there around the radio to listen to songs from local channels that spoke Cantonese. My mother did not care who took the radio away, nor did she join in listening to news from other countries; she pretended she did not know anything. At night, around nine to ten o'clock, my

cousins came to my house and tried to find some channels that were from Hong Kong so they could hear foreign
news or western music such as the *Voice of America*. I was
not interested in the news that adults were interested in.
What interested me were the ghost stories from the Hong
Kong radio broadcast. I put my radio on my bed and heard
the music and ghost crying; it made me shiver in delight. I
would use my comforter to cover my head, our small house
crowded in the afternoon and at night. My cousin came to
sleep over; their goal was to listen to the ghost story, which
always started at 11:00 P.M. Of course, we always sounded
the alert if any guard might come by to check on us.

In those days, my third cousin Ruen always asked me
to accompany him to the market by bicycle to sell his crops.
I learned how to sell goods in the market. After that, on the
weekends, I would bring some bananas or cabbages from
our yard and put them in a basket attached to the bicycle to
go to the city with my cousin. We usually woke up very early and rode our bicycles loaded with beans and vegetables
for more than an hour to reach a nearby small city that was
about twenty kilometers away from my home village. We
took our products to a busy street that was close to a draw-
bridge, which opened a few times each day to let the boats
go through. When the bridge opened, a lot of people would
be waiting on that street for the bridge to close again. The
line was almost a mile long; some of the people did not
want to wait, so they would look around for street vendors
to buy something, so my products sold quickly. Although
I was only eleven years old, I could beat my competitors
in the market. Other adults were selling their cabbages for
seven cents per pound. They used to soak their vegetables
in water overnight to get more weight and make them look
fresh. I was selling at the same price without soaking my

cabbages in water. My vegetables looked dry, but the customers were not stupid because they knew I did not cheat, so they all came to my spot.

On a Sunday, Ruen and I went to the same street in the morning just on time for the bridge to open. We moved our bicycles on foot and watched how other people set their prices for their produce. I noticed six or seven people already put their products for sale—some of them selling their bananas for thirty-one cents per pound. I used to sit next to Ruen. Our products were different; he used to sell eggs and chickens, so we did not compete with each other. I took off my basket from my bicycle, which had a burlap bag of bananas in it. I used the bag to hide my products so village people would not see I took the produce to sell it in the black market. I carefully took out my bananas and used the same bag as the mat on the floor so my bananas would not get dirty.

Once I sat on the curb, a young man stopped in front of me and asked, "Hey, kid, how much are your bananas?"

I replied: "Thirty cents per pound." This made my math easy. In those days, there were no calculators or electronic scales that could show the price. I took out an old fashion Chinese steelyard balance scale to weigh the bananas. The man chose a bundle of bananas and put it on my scale. I calculated the total price in my head and said, "Sixty-three cents." He did not believe I could do the math correctly and said, "Show me your scale." I showed him the string position on the rod of the scale, even with the rod tilting up a little, then said: "See, it shows two pounds and one Liang, one Liang is one-tenth of Chinese pound, so it is sixty-three cents."

The guy was convinced I didn't overcharge him.

A middle-aged woman watched us. When the guy

left, she said to me: "Can you sell it to me for twenty-nine cents per pound?"

I told her, "No" because the math would be more complicated. Besides, my bananas had a better look than others' because I learned how to make the banana golden yellow from my uncle. Whenever a bunch of bananas was fully mature on the tree but still green, I cut it down and carefully put it in a big pot. I lit a small piece of wood and inserted it into the banana's stem. Then I covered the pot tightly. That way, a lot of smoke would be kept inside of the pot. A few days later, the bananas became golden yellow. My bananas always sold out fast. Usually, I could earn more than ten yuan in one morning. It made me feel like I was a millionaire because it was almost the same amount as my mother's salary from the commune for two and a half months. After I came back home from the market, I gave all the money to my mother. I was very proud.

One day, Ruen and I were extremely hungry after we sold all our goods in the afternoon. He said, "Let's find a restaurant to eat at."

"Restaurant? I have never been to a restaurant before," I told him.

Ruen answered, "I went to a restaurant with my dad, and we ordered a dish called Big Mix. I want to have it again."

We walked for a while and found that restaurant. I nervously followed him into the small place. There were many male customers there, and instead of sitting, they squatted around the tables. A short, middle-aged man who wore a white cap and held a white towel came in front of us and said, "Hey kids, what do you want to eat?"

Ruen immediately said, "Big Mix!" and I quickly followed, "Big Mix!"

We found a seat to sit down, and soon that man brought a big dish to us. It smelled delicious. There were chopped pig's ears, stomach, intestines, and livers on top of rice covered with a light brown sauce and a few chopped green onions. I had never seen so much meat in one dish before. Since we were very hungry, the taste was absolutely delicious. It was the best food I had ever had! We both held our bellies with a satisfying feeling of satiety. Later Ruen said, "You need to pay me back."

"Oh, how much?"

"One and a half yuan and a half-pound food coupon."

"I don't have a food coupon."

"Just give me the money."

"Thanks!"

From that day on, I loved to bring any kind of vegetables or fruit to sell. I was sure my mother liked what I was doing since she neither stopped me nor encouraged me to go. Whenever I saw pouring rain in the evening on a very hot summer day, I knew that there would be a lot of shrimp flowing on top of the water the following day before sunrise. I would wake up very early the next morning before the shrimp went back to the bottom of the water. I could easily scoop a few pounds of shrimp with a small net to bring the shrimp to sell.

However, selling any product privately was not allowed at that time. Anyone trading anything privately would be accused of engaging in "speculation and profiteering." Or "practicing capitalism." We were supposed to sell the products to the government and buy almost everything from the state-owned stores. Since I was so young, no one took me seriously. The local people just considered me as "an unusual child." I loved to wear short pants in the summertime, which was something the local girls never did. My mother made short pants or a shirt without a collar for me. My clothes made me look very weird since all the people in China wore the same kind of clothing, which looked like an army uniform. My mother did that because she did not have enough fabric to make those clothes. In others' eyes, I acted like a boy. Most of all, I did many "bad things," such as selling goods in the black market that no other girls were daring to do.

One day, one of my older cousins who was working as an accountant for the production team, nervously ran to my house. She gave us the bad news that I was on a blacklist and that I would be sent to a detention center's "study class" for young adults who engaged in private trading, or whose class consciousness was not in line with communist doctrine. Only people who had serious offenses were sent to this class. My mother and my sister panicked because the detention center could be severe punishment, and it would affect my future. I had two older cousins who had been in the "study class"; they were required to sleep on straw in the brigade office, learn Mao's thoughts, do self-criticism, and not be allowed to go home for one to two weeks. But I was too young to realize what horrible thing was waiting for me, so I did not care. After being placed on the blacklist, people called me a "little capitalist trader."

One day, while we were in class at school, the production team office's loudspeaker announced: "All commune members, everybody come to the meeting area now for an important meeting!" I was very nervous. *Are they going to put me in the detention center?* I wondered. Typically, they hold a public meeting to denounce several people before putting them in the detention center. The image of my Big Uncle being beaten up on a stage at the public denouncing meeting immediately sprang to mind.

CHAPTER 25

THE END OF MAO'S ERA

THAT ONE MORNING IN SEPTEMBER 1976, we were called to attend an important meeting by a loudspeaker announcement. I followed all the students in my school to the meeting area. I listened to a radio broadcast from the Chinses Central People's Broadcast station, "Our Great Leader Chairman Mao Ze-Dong has passed away. . . ." Everybody was shocked and nervous. Some of them cried immediately in the meeting; a few of them were pretending because I did not see any tears in their eyes.

After the meeting, we walked back to our class. A girl said, "America will invade us."

Another girl added, "We should keep the secret from foreigners, that way no one will invade us."

Two other girls looked at me with hostility and said, "Her father is in America."

I felt so confused why these girls treated me like an enemy when Chairman Mao had just died; I hadn't done anything. But as always, I had already accepted that I was a persona non grata.

A sequence of memorial services occurred the following days. Other regular activities like the detention center's "studying class" were canceled. So I was lucky to avoid the "study class" in the detention center.

During that time, we were all supposed to wear either black or gray clothing; red clothing was prohibited. My mother always made clothing for us using fabric from Hong Kong. My father thought girls should wear red or pink clothing; therefore, my clothing was very different from the local girls'. My clothing always had some red or pink in it. Therefore, I had no clothing to wear to school during the period of mourning. Luckily, I found a brand-new outfit that my mother had made for my sister that had no red in it. It had a beautiful pattern with green flowers. I wore it to school every day. At the memorial service, during the solemn and respectful dirge, I looked around the whole meeting ground to see that it was thronged with a dense crowd of dark clothing. I was the only one among a few hundred students and teachers who wore shiny new clothing. I felt a little bit embarrassed. After the meeting, a few girls reminded me to wear black.

Behind the people's outward actions of paying respect to the great Chairman Mao, I was perplexed as a child by their actions of extreme grief. Even a child could tell some of their displays were superficial. The adults were confused about their future; their feelings were torn between hope and restlessness. As a result of the Great Proletarian Cultural Revolution, some missed Chairman Mao. Yet some had waited a long time for that day, the day Mao's era ended, especially the ones who had suffered under him. As a "little capitalist trader," I was feeling quite lucky because the detention class was canceled due to Mao's funeral event.

With the country in turmoil, the adults could not wait to learn what would happen to the central government. They were eavesdropping on the news from Hong Kong radio broadcasts every day even though listening to the news from Hong Kong was considered a crime. People did not care anymore because they realized a historical turning point was happening. I was too young to feel that; I went on my way to play while the adults agonized.

Whenever they saw me walking by them, they turned off the radio immediately or told me to go away. The funeral music went on and on every day from the official radio and the loudspeaker in the production team office for at least a month; no one could escape that sad music. It irritated me; I just wanted to ignore it.

One day my cousin Ruen told me secretly that something had happened in the central government. "Do you know Jiang Qing?"

"Yeah. Chairman Mao's wife."

"Do you know? She is a bad person."

"No way."

Ruen tried to convince me that Jiang Qing was a bad person, but I was not interested in his secret news. My reaction wasn't the outcome he had been hoping for. He walked away from me with disappointment. Later he went to tell other students in the school that he had heard the news about Mao's wife Jiang Qing and a few others in the central government who were bad people. The other students reported him to the teacher. He was soon pulled into the vice principal's office. The vice principal questioned him about where he had gotten the news, who had told him, etc. After that, I did not see him for a few days because he was not allowed to go home, and he was confined to the brigade's office for interrogation.

Ruen's family was very worried, and so was I. Everyone in school knew that he was in serious trouble because he was presumed to be an active counter-revolutionary. The village people were gossiping about him. The sky seemed filled with a solemnity. The school stood in combat readiness since Ruen's case was entangled with the top officials' reputation in the central government. Every day after I came home from school, the first thing I did was to go to my cousin's home to check if he had returned. The more I went to his home, the more frightened I was because his mother did not want to eat and just cried. Her eyes swelled like cows' eyeballs. His family had grave concerns not only for my cousin but also for his mother.

Luckily, a few days later, we heard the news from a loudspeaker: "Down with the Gang of Four!" The news was too startling, almost unbelievable. The Gang of Four was the name given to four top Chinese communist officials who were responsible for directly conducting the Cultural Revolution (1966–76) and were subsequently charged with a series of crimes. One of the members included Mao's wife Jiang Qing, so Ruen was immediately released. My cousin heard this news before the Chinese citizens received it because some people in our hometown eavesdropped on news from Hong Kong. The news at that time was usually covered up by the government.

A year after Mao's death, no one called me the "spy girl" anymore. I was a hated pariah and then became a popular girl. I was in middle school and allowed to join different school activities. I had friends come to my house almost every day for a sleepover. No one humiliated me anymore. Even the attitude of my nasty aunt and her son was totally different from before. They treated my family very well. My mother finally could stand up in front of others. I could not remember ever seeing her so happy. Sometimes, she even rode the bike with my older cousins and went out to watch movies or some games. She seemed full of life and engaged in many activities. I felt a lot more relaxed with her. She did not scold me, even when I made mistakes. When a mother is not happy, it can impact her children negatively. I was lucky that I had an older sister and a grandmother who were always there to comfort and protect me. I was glad those unhappy days were over.

Not only did our family have full lives, but other people in the village also became more active, too. In the markets, I saw a lot more merchandise. People no longer used coupons to buy their everyday necessities. There was even a television in the village office where we could go to watch. There was no more "class struggles" propaganda. One time we watched Deng Xiaoping, a reformer who led China toward a market economy, make an official visit to Japan. We were amazed at how advanced other countries were. Ruen said, "You know what? The foreigners say that all Chinese are sleeping right now." He always got some kind of news that I did not know. Eavesdropping on foreign news was very common in those days.

In 1978, my parents communicated with each other more frequently than before. Sometimes I heard the village people gossip about how my mother had finally ended her suffering. The village leaders and the cadres often came to my house, which never happened before Deng Xiaoping took power. The cadres sometimes came as a group, sometimes individually. Every time they came over, my mother offered the best food and rice wine to them, so they drank and chatted until very late at night. If one came individually, it usually meant they wanted to borrow some money from my mother. They knew that my father sent money to us from America quarterly. It appeared as if my mother treated them better than us because some of the food was expensive at that time. I wondered why my mother was so nice to them. Later, I learned the reason. We needed those local cadres to stamp our official documents because we were in the process of getting passports to leave China. With all her miserable past experiences in her life, she was very careful about how she treated the local cadres. She said, "Deng Xiaoping's policy was good, but the local villains were hard to deal with."

CHAPTER 26

LEAVING CHINA

ON JANUARY 9, 1979, in the early morning before dawn, my mother, my sister, and I left our home village. My mother held a plastic handbag. That handbag had some important documents such as birth certificates, marriage certificates, and other proof from the local office; it also had a small amount of soil from our yard. She took only a plastic handbag without any other luggage, so we would not catch anyone's attention when leaving our hometown before sunrise. Even at that moment, she did not tell me that we would not come back because her documents were not all approved by the authorities yet.

I remember the afternoon vividly before leaving; my mother came back home from the village office and talked to herself, "We came here like a rainstorm, and we are going to leave here like dust." I looked at her holding a document, which was a resident's book, and she said, "I made years of effort with so many hardships to get these residence certificates for the three of us, and today I spent less than two minutes to cancel them." She then looked at me a moment and told me that I could not go back to school anymore because she had canceled our resident permits already. I was perplexed by her expression. I just stared at her with my mouth open as if I had a thousand questions to ask. After dinner, she took a piece of cloth, dug up a little earth, and carefully wrapped it.

"Mama, why are you doing this?"

"No matter where you go, always remember where

you came from."

I felt adults were weird. I just wanted to walk away. She said to me, "I don't know if we are going to come back here or not. By the way, you need to go to your school right now and get a letter from your principal to prove your grade in middle school. You may need it in the future."

It was a surprise to me. I knew that I might go to the United States sooner or later because my father was there, but not this soon. I stood there like a log and looked at my mother, but she seemed busy talking to my grandmother. My mother looked at me and added, "Oh, it's late right now, so you can ask your older cousin Ah Lian to go there with you." I was baffled and asked her, "What should I tell the principal?" She said, "Just tell him that you are going to go to America and need a document from him to prove that you are a middle school student, but don't tell him that you are going to leave tomorrow." My mother chose to do this last minute because she did not want the village people to know.

Ah Lian was not only my cousin, but she was also my classmate. She accompanied me to the school. It was very dark since the sun set early in January. There were no streetlights in the countryside; we could barely see the road. Finally, we reached the school. The principal was still in the office with another teacher. That teacher was from the city, so she had no home in the village and lived at the school as the principal did. When my cousin and I arrived, they were very surprised. I guess I was the only student who went to his office that late at night. The principal smiled at me and asked, "What's going on? Why have you come here?" I told him what I wanted, and he was happy to do it. He tore a piece of paper, divided it in half, and started to write on it. Next, he took a stamp and carefully stamped it on the paper. After he finished, he held up that paper and was very proud. He said, "Ha! This paper can go to America!" The other teacher looked at him and said, "I don't know how she can survive there. She cannot speak any English." I came home with that piece of paper from the principal and told my mother what the other teacher said to me. My mother was very firm and said, "I don't care as long as we can be reunited with your father."

After I came back from the principal's office, my sister and I started to pick out our best clothing for the next day, which was our usual way of going to Guangzhou City. We carefully put the clothing next to our pillows. We were a little excited, so we did not want to go to sleep. It was unbelievable that I did not feel I was going off to a distant place. I felt like I could come back within a few days, so I did not feel I would miss anything. It was late, and my grandmother urged us to go sleep, so we did. Early the next morning, at about 4:00 A.M., my mother woke us up. We quickly dressed and found out my mother and grandmother had made a big meal overnight. Looking back, I guess they did not sleep at all. A whole cooked chicken was put in front of the ancestor's altar. My mother lit the incense and asked us to prostrate to our ancestors and God in heaven. Then we started to eat; a few very close relatives came in the early morning to join us. My grandaunt held my hands and looked at me from head to toe and said, "Oh! How nice! Finally, you can see your daddy again." She then went to talk to my mother.

After the meal, around 5:30 A.M., we didn't clean our dishes because my grandmother urged us to leave. Some relatives wanted to go with us, but my grandmother stopped them because she did not want us to attract attention. She was worried that the local villains, like some of the cadres, might block us on the way because some of them could be hostile, and some of them were simply jealous. Therefore, she only allowed my Big Uncle, who was always a good decision maker, two other cousins, and herself to go with us. On the road, my teacher, Mr. He, who gave all the candies back to me on the International Children's Day, rowed a boat over and asked me where I was going. I simply replied to him that I was going to go to Guangzhou City. He looked at us with a sad expression. I felt terrible that I did not tell my favorite teacher our final destination, but my mother exhorted me not to tell any-one that we were heading to the US. My favorite dog, Julai, seemed to understand what was going on; she followed us for a few miles to the bus stop. I told her, "Julai, go back!" She didn't move. When the bus came, and we were getting on the bus, Julai tried to follow us. My grandma told her to stop, and the bus door closed in front of her. Through the window of the door, I saw Julai's big eyes watching me with great sadness. The bus moved, and I watched Julai follow behind the bus. The bus drove away faster and fast-er, and Julai's little body finally disappeared in the morn-ing fog. My eyes were foggy because of my tears.

It was a beautiful hometown, and I had so many child-hood memories there!

Our whole group took the bus and rushed to our county government to get some documents. My mother had been in this office many times when she applied for resident permits. She waited outside of the office nervously. All her memories came back like a movie: no resident permits, no money, no food coupons. She had been just a social pa-riah distrusted by officials and scorned by neighbors and relatives because of the title of my father. Soon a person came out of the office, and he signaled my mother to get in. My mother held her plastic bag and walked in fearfully. Once she stepped into the office, she was surprised that the person in the office was Wanwang Luo, the one who had helped her to get the countryside resident permits for us. My mother felt a little bit relieved but remained alert and vigilant. He pointed to a chair and asked my mother to sit down. He said slowly, "Tell me the truth, how did your husband go to Hong Kong? Did he escape there or did the government give him permission to go there? If you don't tell me the truth, I am not going to stamp any of your documents." My mother was scared and broke out in a cold sweat; she almost cried out but tried to control her emotions. Her head felt like a lightning bolt struck her, and she did not know whether she should lie or tell the truth. If she lied, sooner or later, he would find out that her husband escaped to Hong Kong. If she told the truth, she might get into big trouble.

My mother knew that Luo was not a bad person, but who knew what he was thinking? What if he refused to stamp her documents? Then she would never meet her husband again. She looked at him with a nervous repugnance of his question, which she tried to subdue. My mother spoke nervously and with quivering lips. She said quietly, "My husband escaped to Hong Kong." After all the fear that he put on my mother, Wanwang Luo didn't say anything, and he stamped her documents. My mother held her documents tightly and walked out of that office like a ghost was chasing after her.

Afterward, we immediately took another long distant bus headed to Guangzhou City. On the way to the city, my mother seemed worried and excited. She was worried that someone who claimed to represent the government might show up and block our departure. But she was also excited. She had been severely shaken by her experience in her vagrant life and all the struggles she had before, so whenever she got the official stamp on her documents, she felt relieved. We arrived in Guangzhou City in the evening, where Little Aunt Guijing was waiting for us. We stayed at her home for the night. The next morning my mother immediately went to the governor's office to get the passports. In 1979, China had just started the policy to allow private citizens to go to foreign countries, so only a very limited number of Chinese people could get a passport. We got our passports quite smoothly in Guangzhou City. Then my mother immediately took us to have a medical exam, which was required by the United States.

In the afternoon, my mother got all documents to leave China; she carefully put them in her bag and held them tightly for fear of them being snatched away. She had a surge of happiness and excitement. My sister and two other cousins were curious and wanted to see the documents. My mother said, "No, not here." Seeing her shaking hands, Big Uncle smiled with a lightened heart and reminded my mother to go to a telephone company to make a long-distance call to a relative in Hong Kong.

My grandmother came to me and said, "Ah Jade, come back to see me if you can. I am always waiting for you."

"Of course. I will come back soon."

"No, you are going to America. It's far away!"

"You mean I won't see my Julai and Slow Feet anymore?

"Don't worry, I will take good care of them."

There was such sadness in leaving a person who loves you so strongly and whom you love right back, but it was my time to leave her. In the evening, my mother, sister, and I sent Big Uncle, grandmother, and two other cousins to the bus; my grandmother turned her head to us and extorted my sister and me to be good daughters to Mama and Daddy. Her eyes watered with tears, but she still smiled.

She looked at my mother and said, "Ah Zhen, if you get homesick in America, or you don't get accustomed to the water there, then boil the water with the home soil, it will cure your problem."

"I will. I know how to take care of myself. Rong is there. Take care of yourself."

At that moment, I realized why my mother brought the soil with her. As I watched my grandmother, Big Uncle, and two cousins depart, all the memories gathered up in my chest: The Pearl River, the canal, and all my animals flashed in front of my eyes. Since I could remember, my grandma had always been there for me. The reason I could go through so much misery and mistreatment in my childhood was because I always felt the big love and protection from my grandma. While the bus was leaving I felt part of my soul imprint onto my grandmother's body and go home with her.

CHAPTER 27

FAMILY REUNION IN HONG KONG

"Ah Jade!" my mother shook me the next morning. I
opened my eyes and saw my mother looking over her documents in her plastic handbag. It was a small bag about
the size of a modern plastic shopping bag. She didn't pack
any clothing or any other items for the "big move;" the
plastic bag was our only luggage! Little Aunt Guijing stood
next to her to review the documents one last time: passports, birth certificates, vaccinations, and others. When
finished, my mother put the soil that she dug in her hometown and wrapped it with paper into the handbag. This
soil was the only souvenir of our home village. "We are
leaving soon!" my mother added while hiding her passport and three train tickets in a folded piece of paper. My
heart sped. Even at fourteen years of age, I understood
today was a big day. Everyone's face carried a tight look
though the adults pretended everything was okay. When
Little Aunt Guijing called us: "Come to have breakfast!"
her voice sounded shrill instead of light. Her daughter and
my sister had already put all my favorite dishes on a table:
sausages, roast peanuts, and porridge. I sat down excited-
ly. I scooped porridge into my month and reached for a
sausage.

Maybe this will be a good day, I thought. The nuts
crunched in my mouth from the porridge. There was so
much food I wondered how we could ever finish, but before I finished my first bowl, my mother said: "We have
to go now!" Three cousins, who were my Little Aunt's son

and daughter, and a son of my Big Aunt, accompanied us to the train station.

The son of Big Aunt talked to us through the window.

"I hope I can get on the train." My mother took out all her money and said it to him: "Split this money with your cousins." He did not want to accept it, but my mother told him: "We could not use Chinese money after leaving China." Soon the train started to move, and my cousin's hands still held onto the window. He did not want to let go. A soldier looked at him sternly, so he reluctantly did.

This was my first time on a luxury train. It was a thrill; the trains I had taken before had no seats—everybody sat on the floors, the floor was black. My mother told me that this was because the train had transported coal before. This one was very clean, and each person had an assigned seat. My mother, sister, and I sat together on a soft, four-person seat with a table. We were the only mainland Chinese in the car; all others were from Hong Kong. I climbed over my sister to get close to the window. Outside, acres and acres of flat farmland time sped by; there was not much to see. Even so, it was exciting. I had never traveled so fast. I pointed at something. By the time my sister looked, it was gone!

In about an hour, there was food service offered on the train. Some people ordered roast chicken and roasted sweet potatoes. Of course, my mother didn't order anything because she had no money. The people at the table next to us looked like college students from Hong Kong taking a vacation on winter break. They ordered a lot of food, sang, and played games. Shortly, a few train attendants in blue uniform came, cleaned their tables, and moved all the chicken bones, sweet potato skins, and other leftovers to our table. Our table was piled up with the leftovers for a few hours. I felt intimidated by the train attendants. The way my mother looked down and refused to meet anyone's eyes added to my sense of inferiority.

One of the young guys at the next table asked a female train attendant: "Where are we now?"

She politely responded: "This is Shenzhen." She seemed to treat the Hong Kong people on the train as privileged. I looked through the window; it was still dark farmlands with a few houses here and there. Today, Shenzhen has become China's newest major city with thousands of tall buildings.

The train stopped at the Luo-Hou Bridge station, which is at the border of Hong Kong. Everybody got off the train. We followed the crowd, walking in a hallway toward the Chinese border security checkpoint, which was a heavily guarded building. The line was long; we waited there for about three hours. My legs were exhausted, so I sat on the floor. I looked around the building, there were about forty people in the room, and two soldiers were standing by the entrance door. A slogan—LONG LIVE THE GREAT FRIENDSHIP OF THE PEOPLES OF THE WORLD!—was written on the wall.

Finally, it was our turn; two customs officers checked my mother's documents thoroughly. One of them said: "You are going to America? Do you have any relatives in the US?"

"Yes, my husband lives there."

"Do you have more documents to prove it?"

My mother handed him out a letter in English written by my father with an official seal. None of us could read English. The officer walked to a back office with the letter. While we were waiting, there was a family of four; a couple with two young teenage sons had been turned back.

I saw my mother looked more nervous; it made me feel my heart pounding faster. Finally, an old man came out with the English document. He told the officers that we could go, but an officer still asked my mother where we would stay in Hong Kong; my mother answered without hesitation, "Number Five Alliance Building, Da Pu Boulevard, Kowloon." We passed the Chinese border security; I looked at my mother, she smiled at us and reached for my sister's hand and mine. It surprised me. She seemed lighter than she had the past few days, and three of us walked across the short Luo-Hou bridge spanning the small river that divides the mainland and Hong Kong. The bridge was small; it was like a regular street. Both sides of the bridge were covered with big boards so I could not see outside. I could barely see water under the bridge through the small gaps in the floor decks. After crossing the street, we walked straight into a building that was the British border control point.

Once we passed over the Luo-Hou bridge, the gate of Hong Kong, we waited in line again to pass through a British customs checkpoint. My mother breathed a sigh of relief. "We made it!" she said with a soft smile. She seemed so relieved. She beamed down at us. From my memory, this probably was the first time I saw my mother smile. Since we left our home village two days before, she had intense anxiety and worry about not being able to leave China. We stood in a long line at the customs checkpoint. After a long wait, we finally passed through, then got on another commuter train to go to Kowloon, which was part of Hong Kong. After another one or two hours' ride, we arrived at Kowloon.

We got off the train, and I saw people going up a long stairway. I felt drained with the whole day of travel; my body still felt like it was on the moving train. But when we followed the crowd to get closer, I realized that I had stepped on a stairway that could move by itself. I was excited since I had never used an escalator, but I was also scared, so I held tightly to my mother's hand. I saw a lot of people behind a railing at the top of the escalator, waiting to meet people coming off the train. When I reached the end of the escalator, a young female stranger suddenly grabbed my hand, turned her head toward an older woman sitting on the floor against the wall, and said, "I think these three people are yours!"

The old woman immediately stood up and ran to us. She asked my mother, "Are you Ah Zhen?"

"Yes."

A tear ran down the old woman's face. Shaking with excitement, she held my mother's hands and said, "Finally, all three of you have arrived safely!" The woman, Mrs. Chu Jian, was in her sixties and was my father's neighbor in Hong Kong. They had become very good friends. When we arrived in Hong Kong, my father was still on the flight from the US to Hong Kong. He asked Mrs. Chu Jian to pick us up at the train station that morning.

My mother asked my sister and me to greet Auntie Chu. We called out, "Auntie Chu!"

Auntie Chu had taken time off from work to go to the train station that morning. She was told that our train would arrive around noon, so she stood in the designated area to wait for us. She stood there for the whole afternoon and still could not see us; then she grew very nervous. She even used a payphone to tell her boss, asking permission not to return to work in the afternoon. Her boss said not to worry. She waited until the evening, and she still had not seen us. She was extremely worried and talked to the people around her who were also waiting, describing to them what her friends looked like so that each of them could help her look for us.

One person told Auntie Chu that we might have been kidnapped by human traffickers on the road. She added, "Your relatives are from the countryside. They don't know anything about the outside world. They are all young women. Think about that: the mother is about mid-thirties, the two daughters are teenagers—they can be sold for a good price." When Auntie Chu heard that, she panicked. Her body sweated, and her legs weakened. Another younger woman next to them comforted her and said the other woman spoke nonsense. Auntie Chu asked the young lady to look out for us while she sat on the floor against the wall. Finally, we arrived in Hong Kong later that evening and met Chu.

Entering the city center in Hong Kong, I saw the neon lights displayed from the tall buildings and stores along the busy streets with cars, two-story buses, and many pedestrians. The flashing light and the noise from vehicles dazzled me. I was nervous about crossing a street with so many cars. I felt bewildered, excited, and exhausted because I hadn't eaten or drunk anything for a whole day.

That night, we stayed at Auntie Chu's place, which was a small studio unit. The unit was made by removable wall panels that divided the whole building floor. There were many small units on the same floor, so it was very crowded. Since there were small gaps between the top of the wall panel and the ceiling, it was very noisy. It was weird that I did not feel hungry even though I hadn't eaten anything since breakfast. I had a bowl of porridge and a few vegetables before I stopped eating. At night, my sister and I squeezed on top of a bunk bed, which was very common in Hong Kong. My mother slept under us. I could hardly fall asleep because of the loud noises of many people playing Mahjong.

The next morning Auntie Chu wanted to take us to a restaurant for dim sum. My mother did not want her to spend money on us. She said, "A simple breakfast is good for us; because the kids had an empty stomach for a day, a big meal is not good for them." So we stayed at home to have soy milk.

After eating, Auntie Chu said: "Sorry, I cannot accompany you to look around today. I need to go back to work."

My mother was anxious to see my father. My father was still on the flight from America and would arrive that evening. So she said, "Don't worry about us. We'll just stay home."

For me, I could not wait to go out to see the strange world. "Can I go out to play on the street with my sister?" I asked my mother.

My mother said, "No."

I argued. "Cousin Ruen said Hong Kong is a free world! Why can't I go out?"

Auntie Chu said to me: "Yeah, free, but it is not safe for you. Someone may steal you and sell you!" I was shocked. I thought that in China, stealing one litchi fruit or selling a chicken or a banana was a crime; how could someone steal a kid and sell a human in Hong Kong? Hong Kong was really free for everything?

I still clearly remember when I met my father for the first time. We were in Auntie Chu's place. She was talking about my father, and my mother listened curiously and quietly. Suddenly the doorbell rang. Auntie Chu stood up and said, "Brother Rong is here." My mother ran to the door, and my sister followed. I was way behind. A kindly middle-aged man stood in the doorway with rolling luggage; he wore a dark gray suit with a tie, neat hair, and shiny shoes. My mother ran in front just wanting to say something, my father spoke out first, "Ah Zhen! I finally . . ."

"Rong!" My parents were so emotional that they could not speak.

"Brother Rong! I am so happy to see you! Today is your family reunion day!" Auntie Chu said.

My father glanced at everyone with a gentle smile. Later his eyes set on me. My mother asked me to call him "Ba Ba." At that moment, I refused and then hesitated, but he smiled at me. My mother poked me a few times and told me, "This is your daddy," so I called out with a very low voice, "Ba Ba." He was very excited and hugged me and held me high, then swung me around. I almost wanted to push him away; he probably felt my expression was not happy; he dropped me down and said, "She used to be a baby, and now she is such a big girl!" while spreading his left hand away from the right showing how little I had been.

My sister walked to him and called out, "Ba Ba."

"Ah Sue, you are seventeen years old. I didn't do my duty as a father for all these years."

"You are always my best daddy," my sister replied.

"You are a sensible child," my father said.

"She always protects her sister," my mother added.

My father was amazed that we could get out of China so fast. He was so excited to meet us. My parents talked nonstop to each other. I did not know my mother could talk so much. She was like an entirely different person around this man I was told to call Ba Ba. I did not know how to act. I felt happy, confused, shy—all at the same time. While my parents spoke, I pretended to look away, but I stole peeks at my daddy every time I thought his eyes were off me.

I could tell that he was very happy and proud. Whenever he met his friends, he always had a big smile, told his friends that he had two daughters and how excited he was to reunite with his family. Whenever we needed to cross the street, he held my hand. I felt quite uncomfortable since he was still like a stranger to me.

The next day, my father's best friend, Wu Lin, who had separated from my father during their escape, invited us to stay at his home, a single house on the hill of Kowloon Tang, where there was a garden and a basketball court in his community. The place was lovely and very quiet compared to the apartment building.

Uncle Wu took at least a week off to accompany us. The first day, he and my father took us to a big department store; I was amazed by the huge size of the store with all kinds of clothing. My mother, sister, and I followed them and took the escalators a few times to reach the floor for all the women's clothing. I looked at the price tags—all of the clothing was expensive when I calculated back to the Chinese yuan.

A lady came up to us and asked politely, "May I help you?"

"Just choose all the clothing that fits the ladies." Uncle Wu pointed at the three of us.

First, the lady showed us the clothing that she thought would fit us, but we were like people who were hard of hearing. My father said, "Just listen to the lady. She will introduce the fashions to all of you." We were still quiet.

"Lady, bring them to the changing room, and you just bring the right clothing for them to try on," Uncle Wu said.

The lady brought us to the changing room; they all had mirrors from different angles.

Wow! What a room, I thought. I looked around and saw my back moving with me. It was the first time I could see myself front and back at the same time. My sister looked at her two long braids that she was proud of that grew to her butt. Even my mother looked at herself and made up her hair nicely. Soon the lady brought so much clothing to the dressing room; I picked an outfit that I thought fit me; after I put it on, I burst out laughing. It was so open; I could see my shoulder! My sister was laughing also. My mother also tried on clothing that was a little bit country styled. I felt those clothes were too expensive, so I chose two blouses, one pair of pants, and one skirt. My sister also chose two sets, but my mother only picked up one suit for the winter. She warned us,

"Ah Sue and Ah Jade, each of you just pick one set, okay? This clothing is too expensive."

We were disappointed, but Mama was right; if she worked one whole year in China she still could not afford to buy one set of clothing here. We walked out of the dressing room; the lady was talking to Uncle Wu and my father, they all smiled at us.

"Got everything you want?" my father said.

"Yes," we all replied at the same time.

The lady saw that each of us only held a set of clothing. She was very disappointed. She talked to my father: "Your daughters are beautiful; if they used make-up a little bit, they'd look like angels. Your wife is so beautiful. They should try more fashionable outfits."

The lady showed each piece of clothing to Uncle Wu and my father; she put the clothing in front and back of my sister and me; she kept saying this one was good, that one fit. My sister and I looked at my mother.

My mother said, "They are too expensive. We don't

need this much clothing."

"As long as my daughters are happy, then I will buy it!" my father said.

My sister and I were very happy; we thought Daddy had a lot of money; each of us chose three sets, my mother chose two sets. The lady was pleased. Before we left, she suggested we buy shoes. Five of us went to the shoe department; I did not buy them because the heels were too high.

Then Uncle Wu and my father brought us to a different shoe store; the heels on those shoes were not that high; each of us bought a pair of shoes. Then we went to a hair salon. People in there treated us like aliens. They gossiped:

"They are from China," one lady said.

"Look, that girl's two long braids. They probably just got here."

"Help them make a fashion statement," Uncle Wu said to the hairdresser.

A woman came out. "Yes, I promise they will look nice. Come with me," she said sweetly.

It was the first time that I got a haircut in a hair salon. After the haircut, I looked in the mirror at my new hairstyle, which was similar to a local Hong Kong girl's short hairstyle without braids. I felt like I was a stranger. The lady asked if my sister could donate her long hair to a nonprofit organization. My sister had no idea that the hair could be donated.

My father said, "Yes."

The next day, we were shopping again and bought three Citizen watches. When a neighbor saw us with the newest clothing, shoes, hairstyles, and watches on our arms, she said: "You have two beautiful 'thousand gold' nieces!"

Uncle Wu looked at us and said, "I am going to broaden your knowledge about the world outside China."

My father replied, "Don't spoil them."

Uncle Wu brought us to a fancy restaurant on the top floor of a very tall building. When we walked in, a man brought us to a big room; from the window, we had a view of the whole of Hong Kong. Two waiters were waiting for us. They stood at attention like soldiers, but they also winked at us. Soon, fancy dishes were put on the table by the waiters who announced, one by one, the fancy names of each dish. Those dishes looked so beautiful, like pieces of art, that I was not courageous enough to eat them. But Uncle Wu scooped a beautiful piece into my bowl and said, "My lovely niece, try it." Oh, no, I was a little upset; how could he destroy the beautiful art? While we were eating, the two waiters stood next to us and served us the food and soup and held the wine bottle to serve my uncle and my father. I felt uneasy with someone watching me all the time while I was eating. I accidentally dropped a napkin, but when I tried to pick it up, one waiter beat me to it while another waiter replaced a new napkin for me. It was awful! They treated me like I did not know how to use my hands. It was the most spectacular dinner of my life. Even today, I still remember the beauty of the eye-opening dishes, but I don't remember the taste of those dishes, and I still feel that the "Big Mix" dish I ate with my cousin in the small, crappy restaurant in China was the best meal I'd had so far.

While we were eating, Uncle Wu said, "Brother Rong, now you have a wife and two grown-up daughters. You don't know how much I admire your family. I am still single, and now I am old. I don't know who would be willing to marry me."

My father replied, "Don't worry, Brother Wu, there must be a nice woman waiting for you right now, and in the future, when you have children, make sure you make their last name Lin, not Chen. That way, your children can carry on your ancestral name."

"I got used to Chen already," Uncle Wu replied.

"We all used fake names when we were vagrants. At that time, we had no choice, but now you are in Hong Kong."

My first impression of Uncle Wu was that he was very charming. He had a gentle voice and was an amiable person to talk to. He treated my sister and me like his own children. Although I had never met him before, I knew a little bit about him since he sent us books from Hong Kong. In 1977, China restarted the university entrance examination after the Cultural Revolution. Many young people were thirsty to receive education again after it had been abandoned for ten years. My sister was only in the first year of high school at that time. She knew that the only way she could go back to Guangzhou City was to get into a college. She wrote a letter to Uncle Wu saying that she thought the hope of getting into college was very slim since she lived in the countryside. Uncle Wu immediately sent her the study guides for the college entrance examination.

Uncle Wu and my father seemed to have never-ending conversations. Many of their friends advised my father and Uncle Wu to go back to China and have a look since China had just implemented an open-door policy. The reason their friends encouraged them to go was that my father already took a long flight from America and could spend a few more hours to go home and visit. They also advised Uncle Wu to go to China to find a woman to start a family, but the two of them did not dare to go back. Instead, we took a long bus ride to the border of China and Hong Kong to gaze out over our homeland.

The two of them were very emotional once they got there; their mood was very heavy. In the beginning, both of them were a little reticent. I did not know what they were thinking about. They stared at the mountains on the other side of the strait, which was mainland China. Later, my father pointed to the mountains and said, "That is Wutong mountain. I have walked through each of those peaks."

"Many have died there," Uncle Wu replied in a heavy tone.

"Many of them were buried there without names. Their families would never find out how they died." My father let out a long sigh.

"Eagle Month Cliff is over there," my father pointed out.

"I saw a few escapees die there at night," Uncle Wu said.

"I saw a person drown while swimming over there," my father pointed to a place on the water.

Their conversation made my heart drop. I had heard so many stories about people escaping to Hong Kong; I thought they all reached Hong Kong and got rich. This was the first time I encountered the truth and heard about the horrible scenes described by first-hand witnesses. My father looked at us and said, "Ah Jade and Ah Sue, do you know how many times I have tried to escape to Hong Kong? Seven times!" His voice rose louder when he emphasized, *seven*.

Uncle Wu said, "We were still the lucky ones who

came to Hong Kong alive!"

My father pointed to my sister and me. "You two are very lucky that you can take the train to come to Hong Kong."

"Now you know what we have been through in order to get here," Uncle Wu added.

I looked at my mother as she lowered her head and seemed to think of something that happened a long time ago.

Uncle Wu recited a poem that meant: "Although my motherland is only a few hundred feet away, when could I step in? You should understand the heart of a man who is residing in a place far away from home." For them, China seemed within sight but beyond reach. For me, all I saw was the empty mountains with some trees. That was nothing compared to my beautiful hometown, but it was too far away to see.

After that, we headed to Uncle Wu's older brother's home; he lived alone. We called him Uncle Shu. He was also a very good friend of my father's older brother when they were young. During the Land Reform Movement, their three mothers—Uncle Shu's mother, Uncle Wu's mother, and their father's third wife—all committed suicide in one day. China's old society had the tradition of polygamy before the communists took over China. Uncle Shu escaped to Hong Kong during the Land Reform Movement and soon lost contact with his family in China. Living in Hong Kong by himself was very lonely, so he thought about his family sadly, knowing most of his family was gone. He tried his luck to see if he could find any family members in Hong Kong, so he advertised in a local newspaper in the missing people section year after year, hoping a miracle would occur. One day, Uncle Wu was eating lunch in a restaurant with a coworker. While reading a newspaper, his co-worker suddenly asked Uncle Wu if a notice in the classified section was his relative or not. Uncle Wu immediately took the newspaper over and read it carefully. He could not believe that his older brother Shu was in Hong Kong. Only two of them from their huge family were able to survive and reunite in Hong Kong. The miracle occurred. When my father and the two brothers got together, they were overwhelmed with emotion, they laughed, they cried.

Uncle Shu had lived in Hong Kong for a long time. He and a few partners owned the biggest temple in Hong Kong at that time, and his temple needed renovation. Uncle Shu asked my father and Uncle Wu to renovate the temple since they had very good reputations in construction work. My mother was very happy; she wanted to stay in Hong Kong instead of going to America immediately since she could not speak English and worried that she could not communicate with people in a foreign country. She persuaded my father and Uncle Wu to accept the job. At first, my father felt the price was very good, but later my father rejected the offer. He told Uncle Shu "I really appreciate your offer, but I need to bring my daughters to America to learn English as soon as possible so that they can get back to school in the US. Children learn a new language and adapt to a new environment much easier than adults, so I don't want to delay them."

Uncle Shu said, "Your daughters' education is important. I understand."

We stayed in Hong Kong for about two and half months. On March 19, 1979, we got on a plane headed for the United States. I was fourteen years old.

CHAPTER 28

STARTING A NEW LIFE IN THE USA

MY FIRST IMPRESSION of our new home in Brooklyn, New York, was a surprise. The one-bedroom apartment was quite empty, with only an old sofa bed in the living room. It did not look like a family's home and was smaller than Uncle Wu's single-family house in Hong Kong. I heard that the sofa bed was picked up from the street by Uncle Hong. Since Uncle Hong came from Hong Kong a few months later than my father, he shared the apartment with my father for a while until he got married. He rented another apartment one floor below in the same building. I realized that my father was so generous with friends, and he sent all his money to his family and relatives, keeping very little for himself so that his lifestyle was incredibly frugal.

In the beginning, my sister missed China so much that she cried because she could not speak in school, and she wanted to go to work with my mother in a sewing factory in Manhattan's Chinatown. My father was very patient and told my sister how important it was to get an education. Not being able to speak the language was only a temporary problem if she studied hard. He said that "Mommy and Daddy were happy to do everything for you."

For me, I really missed my grandmother, my friends, my furry friends, and especially the canal next to my house. When I was a child, I dreamed one day I would live in a tall building so I could look far away. Finally, I had the chance to live on the sixth floor, and all I could see was another building and a busy street. I realized how disappointed I was.

My father seemed to understand our feelings; he tried to make us happy. He brought us to a furniture store. I liked one of the sofa beds very much and pointed it out to my parents. They saw the price tag, which was over their budget.

My father said, "Let's buy this one."

My mother told him, "This is too expensive!"

My father replied, "As long as the children are happy, it is worth it."

My parents worked very hard, like most immigrants. My father worked in a restaurant and usually returned home after 11:00 P.M. When he came home, he always had a big smile and tried to find a chance to talk to us. Within a short time, I found that he was a very comfortable person to talk to. I always waited for him to come home before I went to sleep. Whenever I had mathematics and science homework problems that I could not solve, he always solved them for me no matter how late it was. He took us to watch movies when he had time.

My mother worked in the sewing factory in Manhattan. My sister started to work in the same place after school and on weekends. I stayed home to cook for the family. Sometimes on the weekend, my mother asked me to join them. I did not know how to use the sewing machine, so the boss gave me the job of cutting the ending threads. I used to sit with a few very old women to cut the threads. They paid me three cents per cutting one piece of clothing. I was the fastest one among others, probably because I was young and had good eyes. At the end of the day, I could earn up to twenty dollars for nine hours. Twenty dollars!

The boss said, "Ah Zhen has very good kids, and they earn money with her. Others' kids are fooling around."

My mother was proud, but I did not like work in the factory at all due to the noise and the crowded room. So I quit that job and took my second job of cleaning Chinatown streets with a bunch of other kids and earned three dollars and fifteen cents per hour. A year later, I worked in the Society Security Office in Chinatown as an interpreter with my broken English. I continued to work various jobs from high school to college as a cashier in a supermarket, a receptionist in the Bank of Singapore at World Trade Center, a word processor in the Federal Government's Bureau of Labor Statistics, a clerk in Lotus Development Corporation. I did not feel life was hard while working and studying at the same time, but I did not like the crowded subways, crowded streets, and crowded buildings in New York City. I felt like there was no fresh air there. I missed the canal, the water, the fishponds, fields, and the bamboo in my hometown.

In 1980, my younger brother was born. Though we had five people living in a one-bedroom apartment, my parents were extremely happy. My mother was very proud that she had a son. She was a traditional Chinese woman, so having a son was the most important thing for a wife. She had a horrible experience in the past when one of my father's nephews tried to persuade my father to divorce her during her difficult time in China because she only had two daughters. Now she felt that my father would devote his energy to his son instead of sending money to other relatives in China. Although my father was considered a highly educated man with both western and traditional education, Confucianism was deeply in his mind. Having a son was important for the family. But he treated his daughters as well as his son.

My parents had very different personalities. My father always appreciated just being alive. He never criticized and blamed others, not even the Chinese communist government. However, my mother carried her suffering differently; sometimes, even up to the present time, she had nightmares about the residence permit and trembled with fear of a vagrant life, roaming from one place to another. Many years later, she still fears going back to the wilderness; the sight of the mountains and water strikes a chord in her heart. The chilling vagrant life still stayed in her mind. When we went on vacation, we liked hiking in beautiful wild areas with waters and mountain ridges, but she refused to go with us. She was unwilling to remember her rough life; even today, when she recalls it, she still shudders. On the other hand, my father was very excited to join us.

He tried to persuade my mother to go. "Darling, we are on vacation, not vagrants, no one is chasing after us. Why can't you forget that miserable life and enjoy this one with the children?"

But my mother said, "I don't want to repeat our vagrant life again." She could not heal or forget her pain. The abyss of her past miserable life was ingrained in her brain.

My father comforted my mother, and he said, "During the Cultural Revolution, even the Chinese President Liu Xiaoqi and the Army Marshal Peng Dehua were tortured to death, as well as so many ordinary people. We are very lucky to be alive."

CHAPTER 29

VISITING CHINA

In 1986, when I was twenty-one years old, my parents, my five-year-old-brother, and I went back to China to visit our hometown. We arrived in Guangzhou City first. My parents never forgot the people who had helped them. They brought three color televisions, one for my maternal grandmother Po Po and two for my father's two sisters, while we were still using a black-and-white television at home in New York. They brought watches, bikes, and other expensive things to the people who had helped them. My mother worked at least twelve hours a day and saw their money being spent like water. Her heart ached to see so much spending, but she also felt it was worth it. My mother never forgot my father's former employee, Uncle Liangjiang Wu, who let her and her children into his house to rest when she did not have any place to stay. My parents always taught us to be grateful. Their gratitude was not only emotional gratitude to others, but also showed their thanks to others by helping and paying back the people who had helped them.

During their busy schedule in China, my parents brought my brother and me on a special trip to visit their old neighbors in Guangzhou City. They knew that Mr. Yang, who reported my father to the authorities in the past, had an uneasy conscience. My parents wanted to tell him that they forgave him, and everything was history. Unfortunately, the neighbors said that Mr. and Mrs. Yang had died.

A few neighbors were very shocked. They could not imagine my father was still alive. The landlady came out to welcome us into her house. She was surprised that my parents ended up in America. She said, "Rong, I knew you were different from the others, that you could do something big." She told my father what had happened to other neighbors after my parents left. She said, "I got into a lot of trouble because I was a secondhand landlord with a foreign connection. One day the Red Guards came to search the house, and they found a few pairs of high-heeled shoes that were left by the original owner's family. They asked me to report my foreign connection and communications. But I had lost contact with the landlord who never came back to claim his house after he left China in 1949."

My father offered some large US dollar bills to the landlady and told her that since my mother didn't pay the full rent on time, he would make up for it. She didn't feel my parents owed her anything even in the most difficult times, and the house was taken by the government during the Cultural Revolution anyway. My father still handed her two-hundred dollars. Obviously, she was overcome with emotion. She also said that my mother sublet the house to a nasty tenant who was my mother's cousin, the one that called the security and threw us out at night. The neighbors did not like his family because that family thought they were the purest ones under the communist regime. He and his wife usually caused a lot of trouble for other neighbors. I didn't pay much attention when we visited the old neighbors since I didn't remember anything from that house. My heart was in my home village where my grandmother was.

We eventually went back to my hometown village to see my grandmother. We rode a minivan taxi with a lot of gift boxes loaded in the back. On the way to my home village, I imagined what Grandmother was doing. Was she waiting on top of the levee for us with my dog Julai? How did she look? I could not wait to see her. We arrived in my hometown in the evening, and the driver had a hard time finding my grandma's house since there were a lot of changes, and he could not find anybody to ask because people were inside in the wintertime. My mother and I tried to figure out which village entrance was ours. The driver said, "You should come back more. Everything changes each day now." Finally, my mother and I recognized a place that looked like an entrance to our village. There were a lot more houses than before; all of them had at least two floors with a courtyard, two families even parked a car in front of their houses.

"Wow! Some of the families have cars already," my father said.

"I told you. Deng Xiaoping is a great leader, so the people got rich," the driver bragged about the Chinese government. "Where is the house?"

"My grandma's house is a small house, and our house was the smallest one next to it. So look for the small houses," I said.

The driver drove back and forth few times, then stopped in front of the smallest house. We came out of the car, and my mother said, "This is our house!" The yard wall had disappeared, and the longan tree was cut.

The driver asked us, "You sure this is your house, right?"

"Yes," my mother replied.

We unloaded the bags and boxes. We walked to Grandmother's house, which was behind our house. My mother knocked on the door, "Mama, we came back."

The door almost immediately opened. Grandmother looked at all of us and said, "I have been waiting for you every day." She was so excited to see us. She looked older and shorter. I ran to her and hugged her. "You are taller than before." She patted my head. The feeling of being blessed came back to me. That was the feeling I had when I lived with her as a child. Then she turned her head and looked at my father. "Aa Rong, Mama is thinking of you all the time."

"Yes, Mama," my father replied. In China, men refer to their mothers-in-law as Mama just like they do their own mothers.

She turned her head to my little brother and held his hands, "This is my lovely grandson. Can I have a hug?"

Soon all of my uncles, aunts, and cousins came over to meet us. One of my cousins said, "Grandmother went up the levee every day to see if you were coming back."

My Big Uncle came, he greeted all of us, and said, "What a coincidence, today is the exact day you left here seven years ago."

I saw all those familiar faces, the only face missing was my dog Julai. I asked my grandma, "Where is Julai?"

Grandma looked at me with a little hesitation. "Julai was given to a friend."

The next day, Grandma held my hands and showed me the flowers I planted before going to the United States. She tidily arranged the flowers next to the house—they were still in the same pot but neatly trimmed. My cousin Lian came to see me and told me: "Ah Jade, do you know how your dog Julai died? Julai died because she refused to eat and lost a lot of weight after you left her at the bus stop. No matter what grandmother fed her, she just looked at her and refused to eat. After you left, Julai walked to the bus stop every day, rain or shine, and sat there to look for you to come back for weeks. Whenever people got off the bus, she tilted her head to see whether you came back or not."

While my cousin was talking about my dog, tears came to my eyes. My grandmother winked at my cousin and signaled her not to tell me about the dog. My cousin stopped talking when she found out I didn't know Julai was dead and noticed I was in tears.

My grandmother said, "Don't you have other things to tell her? You know she treated her animals like family members."

For weeks, I saw Julai in my dreams: She sat at the bus stop, the wind was blowing her fur from sunrise to sundown; I saw Julai's fur soaked wet under the pouring rain, and she still sat there like a statue of a dog. Even today, I still have the image in my mind when Julai followed us to the bus stop when we left the village. I could still see her sad eyes looking at us riding away in the bus. . . .

My grandma's eighty-first birthday was coming at the beginning of February, so my parents planned a big birthday party in the village. All of the villagers were invited to celebrate her birthday. They came in to help; some brought their woks, plates, and bowls, others brought their tables over and put them in Big Uncle and Grandmother's courtyard. Since there were at least fifty tables, the courtyard could not hold so many; some tables were put next to the street. Some of the helpers built up temporary stoves, each of which had a wok or a soup pot on top. Chefs came from local villages. One of them was my grandmother's godson, who was in the militia that escorted my father back to the city during the Cultural Revolution. I saw my father go to him and shake his hand; they talked and smiled. I had no idea what they were talking about. Big Uncle organized the preparations; he assigned each helper what to do. Second Uncle and his son Ruen came back from the farmer's market with two boats of pork, chickens, and vegetables. Once the boats docked in the canal, my hard of hearing third uncle and a few others went to move the food from the boats to the courtyards. My father came and handed a stack of money to the second uncle to pay for the food. I went to help to carry the food, but they did not let me because I was a guest. Instead, Big Uncle asked me to greet each visitor/guest. I got very nervous because I used to stutter in front of people. When I saw someone I didn't know, I only said "Welcome," then I didn't know what to say, I felt awkward. Soon a few helpers went to the canal and pulled fish from nets. There were three fishnets, each of the nets had at least fifty fish. These were fish bought the day before; they kept them in the canal with the nets. With all the stuff they moved up to the courtyard, there was one animal I could not see—ducks. I asked my old cousin, "Why was there no duck?"

"Well, we have a custom that we cannot use duck to celebrate a birthday."

"Oh, that is new to me. How come I did not know that." I said.

"When you lived here, all of us were very poor. We did not have many chances to eat meat."

"Yes," I replied.

I went back to the courtyard with my cousin; all the people were very busy with preparations. Some were cleaning vegetables; some were cleaning fish, cutting and chopping. One part I did not want to see was killing the animals, so I stayed away from that.

One of my cousins came to me. "Grandma is looking

for you!" So I went to Grandma's house with my cousin.

There were a few seniors already there that wanted to see how I looked. I called each of them, "Grand Aunt Five, Grand Aunt Seven . . ." They all stood up and looked at me like I was an alien.

"She is a big girl right now. She was vulnerable."

"No one could predict life. She was an extremely poor girl, no residence permits . . . now she is an American!" another one said.

My cousin added, "Didn't you know? She is a college student."

Grand Aunt Seven wiped her eyes and kept saying, "Good! Good! Good!"

I remembered that she was the one who asked the leader of the production team to give my mother a job as a commune member when other villagers scolded her.

"Today is my birthday, the happiest day of my life. Talk about something good," my grandmother declared. Soon my little brother ran in with a bunch of kids chasing after him. He became the center of attention in the house.

In the evening, the street became dark because there were no streetlights back then. Big Uncle borrowed an electric generator to light up the street; his oldest son installed it. Soon the whole street was brightly lit. The tables were arranged in the courtyard and the streets neatly; the dishes were placed on them. I saw the leaders from the production team and brigade came in. Big Uncle, my father, and my mother stood in front of the door and greeted each of them. There were about four hundred people who came to celebrate my grandmother's birthday. One couple did not come to help but showed up at dinner time; they were Fourth Uncle and his wife. I used to hate them because they were so nasty to me and my mother; however, on that day, I did not resent them anymore. My parents went up to greet them, but other people looked at them like strangers because nobody liked them. My grandmother, my parents, a few grand aunts, my little brother, and I sat at one table. Next to us was a table with Big Uncle and all the local leaders, one of them my mother's oldest cousin, Damao, from a different brigade. Before eating, everybody stood up and blessed my grandmother; I could tell she was very happy. She kept telling people to eat, but no one picked up their chopsticks until she had one bite of food first. Everybody was chatting, eating, drinking, and the dishes kept coming up.

Soon Damao stood up and gave a speech, "Thanks for coming, everyone, to the celebration of my aunt's birthday. I want to say a few words. It's in my cousin Rong and Zhen's honor that you are here. Everyone at this table knew that it was not easy for their family, that part of the dark history no one would forget. Rong had been in the labor camp for several years, and he did not succumb to fate; he escaped. Ah Zhen had it even harder; she brought up two kids without residence permits. Now they are proud to be sitting in front of us. Thanks for our great leader Deng Xiaoping's policies. Cheers!"

"Cheers!" Everybody stood up, even the children.

He added, "The most amazing thing is that they are still together. Rong didn't forget his wife even when he went to Hong Kong. He supported his families in the good and bad times. Ah Zhen didn't find another man; she could have left her husband so she would not have that damn bad element title, but she didn't. She raised her daughters. Now she even has a son. Congratulations to them! Cheers!"

Everybody stood up and said, "Cheers!"

The party went on and on through the night. I went to sleep before the party ended. The next morning, I heard my mother talking to my father, "It was worth it to spend that much money. Those leaders treated me like dirt before. Now I can stand up straight in front of them."

The next day, my cousin told me, "Fourth Uncle's pig died without any reason. His wife went to consult with a witch to see what was going on. The witch told her their ancestors did not forgive them because she didn't contribute any money and animals to her mother-in-law's birthday. Therefore, the deity killed the pig." I burst into a laugh. "Superstitions never go away, not by the Cultural Revolution, nor by modernization reforms."

The day when we were leaving, my grandmother called me for breakfast. But my Big Uncle's daughter came and called me to go to her house because my parents and my brother were there, so I ate breakfast with them. When it was time to go, my grandmother, uncles, aunts, and cousins came out to say goodbye. Big Uncle told my parents a few times to come back to see him and not bring any gifts. Their lives were good, and they could buy anything they wanted. I hugged my grandmother a few times; she held my hands and did not let me go. "Po Po, take care. I will be back soon." She let go of my hands.

My cousin Lian said, "Grandma is crazy today. She woke up at three o'clock in the morning to cook breakfast for you." I almost cried out but held on to my throat. I felt terrible that I didn't eat her breakfast; instead, I had eaten at Big Uncle's house. I saw her hands waving with tears in her eyes; all others waved their hands until we got in the car. I suddenly thought, *Life is unpredictable, Po Po loves me the most among all her grandchildren, but I am the only one who has to live far away from her!*

I went back to visit my grandmother by myself in 1991, which was the last time I saw Po Po. She passed away a few years after my visit; I didn't go back for more than twenty years. The last time I went back, my hometown had become a modern city. The fishponds, orchards, and paddy fields were all gone. Former farm fields became high-rise buildings, and many new roads were built, with cars everywhere. All the old small houses were replaced by big three-story single homes. I couldn't even find the canal with bamboo; it became mostly an underground water system. The only thing still there was the Pearl River. There was a new huge concrete levee built next to the old one. A big highway was built on top of the new levee that was directly connected to Hong Kong. The old levee became a leisure trail for people to walk. A small pebble path paved on top of the trail is for people who like foot massages after they finish hiking with bare feet. In 2019, a thirty-four-mile-long bridge-tunnel was built, directly connecting Zhuhai, the city next to Zhongshan, to Macao and Hong Kong. In 1979, it took us more than one day to go to Hong Kong; today, the trip is about forty-five minutes. Standing on the concrete pavement, I felt lost. My home village seemed to have evaporated from the earth. I was trying hard to find any trace of my old home village, but all I could find were the shadows of tall buildings.

CHAPTER 30

GRATITUDE

IN 1991, MY PARENTS finally bought a house in Brooklyn. My father loved gardening; soon his tiny garden in the small backyard became a polychromatic wonder. His friends and neighbors loved to come and sit in the backyard to listen to him talking about the turbulence he had encountered in his life. Regardless of the extremely harsh conditions and dangers, horrible mistreatment, failure, pain, or success and happiness, he faced all of them with a calm mind; the roller-coaster of his life made him look at this universe differently. He did not care about fame and wealth; a peaceful life and a happy family with children around him were what he wanted. With his life experience, he understood human nature. Through an age of provoking hatred and madness, he reached a lofty state of tranquility and tolerance. His personality was like the water in the Pearl River, always flowing toward its destiny, the vast majestic ocean. He neither bemoaned the state of society nor pitied the fate of mankind.

One day, my father and I were admiring his flowers in his yard. He said to me, "Why do people complain about their life? Look what nature provides for us. We have everything!"

"Don't you complain about the Chinese government for what you have been through during those political campaigns like the Cultural Revolution? Don't you blame those guards who mistreated you?" I asked him.

"It was turmoil in the whole country, a disaster of society, just like a natural disaster. You might get caught in it, but there is nothing to complain about if you survive," he answered and added: "Besides, we are just ordinary people and can do only ordinary jobs. What do we deserve? Look at those scientists who can shoot a spaceship to the moon. They deserve to be rewarded."

Indeed, he was always satisfied with what he had. He was grateful that nature provided a wonderful world for him to live and enjoy.

My father was always grateful to everyone who helped him in the past. He often mentioned their names to us. He also loved to help others, such as his neighbors. Whenever something had broken in their house, my father would offer help to fix it. He found so much joy in helping others. As the years went by, he got a second name, "Number One," the best in the neighborhood. One day he was doing work on the ceiling and looked straight down. My sister said, "Ba Ba, don't you feel dizzy?" He said that when he was a contractor in Hong Kong, he walked on a beam on top of the twentieth floor without a safety belt and did not felt dizzy or scared at all. He seemed never fearful of anything.

In 2004, my father was diagnosed with liver cancer, and the doctor's prognosis was he had less than two years to live. We were all shocked and devastated, but my father said that all people had to go through birth, sickness, and death. He would just follow with nature, go with what had happened to him. He went through chemotherapy a few times, but the outcome was not optimistic. A later test indicated that cancer had spread. When the doctor asked him to try a new experimental drug, he trusted the doctor, and he said that he would take it as long as it could benefit other people in the future. My father strongly believed that he would be fine. Before taking the experimental drug, the pharmaceutical company had to do all the procedures like a CT scan, computed tomography, biopsies, and a blood test. After all the procedures, they couldn't find any cancer cells. When they redid the biopsy a few more times, the doctors were amazed that he had no cancer cells in his body without taking the experimental drug. It was a miracle! Our family was so happy! We went on vacation to celebrate his full recovery.

I believe God was sympathetic to my father. God wanted my father to enjoy a few more years in this world. Unfortunately, the cancer cells came back in 2006. For the last few years, my father still tried to be as independent as possible. He still cooked for the family, he gardened, and he helped his friends fix their houses. As his health deteriorated more and more, my mother, my sister, and my brother had to take great care of him, especially my sister. She knew our father loved to go to the gym; she accompanied him to the gym whenever she had the time and took him back and forth to the hospital. In the last month of his life, I went to visit him and found that he was very weak already. He still wanted to get dressed to go to the bus station to pick me up and to drop me off at the bus station when I left to go back home. I told him, "Don't come with me to the bus station and take care of yourself." But he insisted on doing it even though he was very weak. I felt so guilty; since I lived in Maryland, I could not take care of him when he was sick in his final years.

My father's last few months of life were spent in and out of the hospital. The last hospital stay was due to an infection after surgery. When I looked at him asleep in the hospital bed, I felt as if a knife was piercing my heart. There were no antibiotics to cure it. The doctors had a meeting with my brother, my sister, and me. They told us that they had tried everything, but they could not save him. They also told me that my father was a very lucky person because they hardly saw a patient that had so many children and friends visit in the hospital.

My father tried to take a walk with me in the hospital hallway; he held a railing and looked at the sunset. He recited a poem, "The sunset is beautiful, merely close to dusk." One of the doctors told us that my father was an extraordinary patient who did not complain at all. He even explained to me that when he touched my father's stomach, he reacted immediately, meaning my father was in great pain, but he didn't say a word. It was unbelievable that he could walk a few days before he died.

His last request was to go home with the family. We did let him come home since there was absolutely no more treatment they could give to him in the hospital. In the last days before he died, he opened his eyes slowly, made a strenuous effort, and taught me, "Be grateful for everything you have." He still thought of sending money to his sisters and cousins, and helping other people. I told him, "Don't worry, our relatives and friends all have money and good lives now." He looked at me and said, "When we drink water, think of its source." These were his last words to me. His heart always flowed with gratitude, and his words ring in my ears all the time. I saw the sentimental attachment to this world from his eyes. Yet he appeared not to want to extend his life because he was suffering. I felt helpless because I was incapable of saving him.

Even though my father lived for seven years after being diagnosed with cancer, his strong mind could not sustain the years of his weakened body. He passed away on September 23, 2011, three months before his eightieth birthday. Had he not died at home, I would not have believed that he was gone. Even after he died, I still searched traditional Chinese medicine for a solution; it took me almost a year to find an herb that might cure an infection of the liver, but it was too late. I could never get my father back. Sometimes I thought another way to comfort myself was to think that my father left this world early so he would suffer less.

Many years passed, my mother has slowly come back to a normal life, but she has more vagrant nightmares after my father passed away. My sister, brother, and I all have very good families. We are not very rich, but we are all satisfied with what we have. My father always appreciated life and taught his children to be grateful. My father is gone, but his spirit will always be with us.

AUTHOR'S NOTE

I DEEPLY MISS my maternal grandmother, who gave me unconditional love, protection, and wisdom for my childhood. I will forever be grateful to both of my grandmothers, who took care of me during my parents' most difficult time. I would like to thank my parents, who gave birth to me, brought me up, and taught me to appreciate everything I have—especially my father, who always taught his children to be grateful. From him, I learned that gratitude leads us to appreciate all things in life and thus brings us joy. I also thank my husband Weimin and my children Xinyi and George, who give me a wonderful family with so much love.

My mother had mentioned to me that our family's story is longer than a book. Yet it is so hard for me to ask the details of what happened to her because all the stories in her life strike a harsh chord in her heart. Most of my father's friends in Hong Kong were the people who escaped from China during the Cultural Revolution. Their stories were soul-stirring. Many of them left their families in China. The vicissitudes of their lives contained joys, sorrows, partings, and reunions.

My family's story reflects those of millions of Chinese people whose lives were shattered during that time. As the old generation rapidly dies off, my generation is getting older. The new generation in China is living in a completely different kind of prospective modern life. My hometown has become a big city with tall buildings, cars, high-speed trains, and shopping malls. The history of the

Cultural Revolution has faded with time and has been gradually lost.

I hope my personal stories will let future generations know that part of history before it's lost in the shadows of those tall buildings. Specifically, for those former landlords, business owners, scholars, and escapees in southern China, many of whom did not survive the Cultural Revolution and never had a voice in this world.

Life goes on. Thinking back about what has happened throughout the past, I believe everything has its own fate. We usually lament that our fates are uncertain; we cannot recognize them clearly, especially when politics intervened in all paths of life. Either some political leaders wanted to promote a utopian paradise or just wanted to obtain their power, they usually rallied their supporters by blaming another group of people. It often creates fear, hatred, and division in society. That will have severe consequences. Nature and humans are connected to each other. After all, all people have a conscience. That is our human nature. To go against nature brings bad consequences. The universe is not only what we see every day, but it is also something we cannot see. What we see all depends on how we feel in our hearts. Life goes on. Our memories go on.

ACKNOWLEDGMENTS

FIRST, I want to thank my husband, Weimin, who helped me write this entire book, turning so many pieces of my scattered memories and broken narratives into a coherent story.

I owe very special gratitude to Connie Paulson, who first encouraged me to write this book when she taught me to write a few English essays.

I thank all my friends who edited my book including Sheauwei Yu, Professor Tiffany Shao, Kenneth Fredrick, Amy Richardson, Bridget MacKillop, and Suzanne Yuskiw.

I really appreciate all the suggestions, comments, and English edits for my book from members of Olney Writer's Group and Northern Montgomery County's Writers Club, including Michele Miller, Andrew Hiller, Bob and Sue Esty, Emily Wood, Bryan Byrd, Mary Lou Williamson , Liza Schor, Mark Ballweg, Kaitlyn Jain, Jerrie Reger, and Linda Meyer.

I thank my publisher, Jeffrey Goldman of Santa Monica Press, who recognized the value of my book, as well as editor Lisa Rojany who performed the final edit.

APPENDIX A

Partial List of Political Campaigns and Movements in China from 1949–1978

1) <u>Land Reform in 1950</u>: This government movement forced the landlords to give up their land and subsequently redistribute it to the poor peasants who had no land. This movement began in 1947 when the communists took over part of China and continued after the communists conquered the whole of China.

2) <u>Campaign to Suppress Counter-revolutionaries from 1950–1953</u>: This political campaign was launched after the founding of the People's Republic of China, the Campaign to Suppress Counter-revolutionaries, aimed to suppress residual opposition, including former Kuomintang's (ruling party of the Republic of China, now settled in Taiwan) remaining underground force of supporters and spy operations. The campaign expanded to suppress functionaries, businessmen, and intellectuals who worked for the former government. Those accused of being counter-revolutionaries were denounced in mass trials; many were sentenced to forced labor or condemned to be executed.

3) <u>Three Anti and Five Anti Campaign in 1951–1952</u>: This campaign was anti-corruption, anti-waste, and anti-bureaucracy in the party, government, army, and mass organizations. The movement was against "five evils," which were anti-bribery, anti-theft of state property, anti-tax evasion, anti-cheating on government contracts, and anti-stealing state economic information as practiced by owners of private industrial and commercial

enterprises.

4) <u>Anti-Rightist Movement from 1950–1960</u>: This An-ti-Rightist Movement, in the 1950s and early 1960s, consisted of a series of campaigns to purge rightists in the country. The definition of "rightists" was not always consistent; it included people who criticized the gov-ernment's communist/socialist policies or expressed disagreement with the government.

5) <u>The Great Leap Forward, 1958–1961</u>: Initiated by Mao Zedong and the communist party, the aim was to rap-idly transform China into a modern communist society. The Great Leap Forward was to revival and catch up the Chinese economy after so many years of WWII, the civil war, and the Korean war by significantly increasing the agricultural and industrial production, and the mod-ernization of Chinese industry and agriculture. Mao announced the goal of surpassing the steel production output of Great Britain in fifteen years. As a result, the whole country was mobilized to produce "steel" using homemade furnaces and hunting all the birds to reduce the grain loss from agriculture. This production took many farmworkers away from their fields. Therefore, agriculture production was affected.

6) <u>People's Commune Movement 1959–1962</u>: Mao initi-ated this movement to accomplish a societal transfor-mation for a Marxist communist society. He directed the formation of People's Communes in the country-side by recombining all the lands which had been dis-tributed previously to the lower-class peasants. This ended the private ownership of land and production tools/equipment in China. Communes were formed, and everything had to be turned over to the collectives. Countryside people became commune members who

had to work together in the field and eat together in the public canteens with tremendous waste because people were not allowed to keep food and eat at home. The government pushed very hard to increase agricultural production and set vigorous competition of grain production between the communes. The local commune leaders significantly inflated the numbers for the harvest, which resulted in turning in all their grain production to the government. The government used those agricultural products to pay off its loan to the Soviet Union. All these resulted in the biggest famine spread across all of China and caused millions of people to die unnaturally.

7) The Cultural Revolution from 1966–1976. The revolution was supposed to change the old culture and old establishment in China. Mao Zedong, who was the Chairman of the Chinese Communist Party, started this movement in 1966. He wrote the first "dazibao," the large poster, to start the Cultural Revolution. He accused government officials of going on a capitalist roadway and the Soviet "correctionism" roadway. He was calling young people to rise up and demolish the establishment (government system) as well as the old culture. As a result, many people, especially students, followed the call and formed "Red Guards" and anti-authority rebel organizations. The country was in complete chaos, with riots everywhere. During the Cultural Revolution, the Chinese president, Liu Shao-qi, among many government officials and military generals as well as many innocent ordinary people, were tortured or even killed at the Public Accusation and Denouncing Meetings. As a result, the Chinese government was totally paralyzed, universities and schools were closed,

factories stopped production. And Mao gained his absolute power in China.

8) *The Destruction of the Four Olds from 1966–1970.* This was one of the first significant measures instituted by Mao Zedong at the outset of the Cultural Revolution. Mao Zedong called for the destruction of the "Four Olds"—old ideas, old culture, old habits, and old customs. Confucious' teachings were considered obstacles to building the new China. The task fell largely on the Red Guards, who carried out Mao's orders to destroy the Four Olds; many artifacts were destroyed and books were burned. People in possession of these goods were punished. The movement continued until Mao's death.

9) <u>Going to the Countryside Movement from 1968–1978</u>. This movement was started to curb the chaos of the Cultural Revolution and to dissolve the Red Guards. The Cultural Revolution had destroyed the economy; therefore, the cities could not support all the young people to provide them with jobs and food. Mao initiated a campaign to send urban youth to remote rural areas to "learn from the peasants." As a result, those youths lost the opportunity to pursue advanced education. It was later called the lost generation.

10) <u>Criticize Lin, Criticize Confucius from 1973–1975</u>. This campaign was against former Vice President Lin Biao, who died in a plane crash while fleeing to Russia after a failed coup against Mao in 1971. It was a political propaganda campaign, started by Mao Zedong and his wife Jiang Qing, the leader of the Gang of Four. The Criticize Confucius campaign was targeting the popular Premier Zhou Enlai, who was hated by the Gang of Four. Zhou Enlai was criticized as representing the reactionary forces of Confucianism.

APPENDIX B

Family Trees

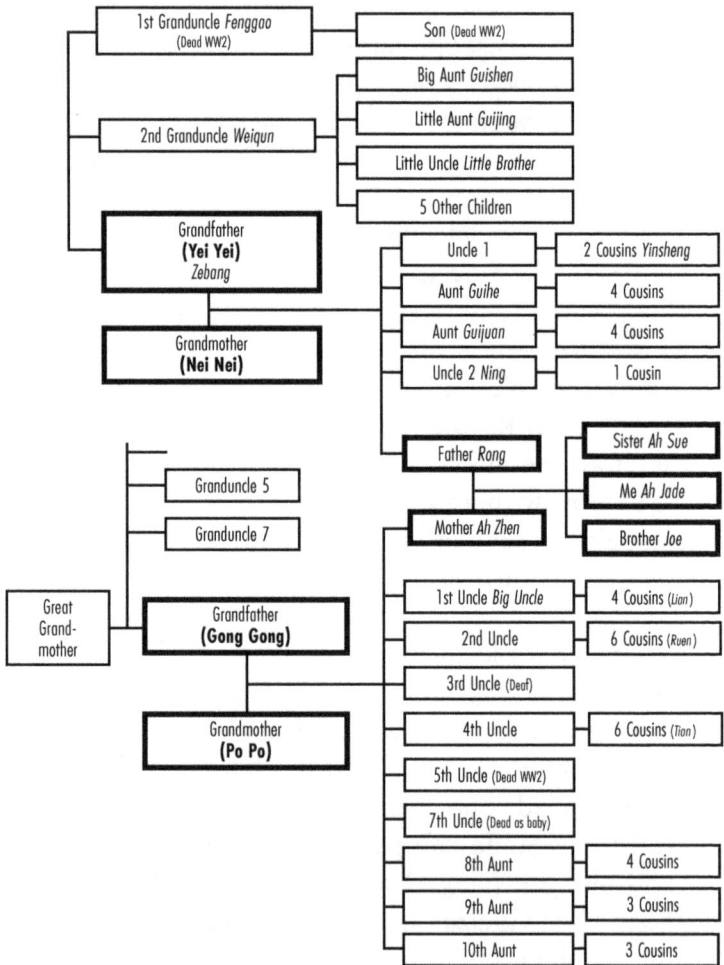

APPENDIX C

The Point System as Labor Salary in the Chinese People's Commune

There were four grades within the labor force. The first-grade force were leaders, the cadres in the village, and the "model workers"; the second level were the strong men; the third level were the women; and the fourth level the elderly and those who had a bad title, like the families of former landlords. The first level of the labor force earned about ten to twelve points per day; the second labor force earned seven points; the third level earned only three to four points per day. One point was worth about 0.04 yuan, depending on how much the village produced that year. In addition, the first labor force received seventy pounds of unprocessed grain per month (which would make forty-seven pounds of rice), the second labor force earned sixty-eight pounds of grain, and the third labor force earned sixty-four pounds of grain. The non-working elders and children earned twenty pounds of grain. That grain was not free; it had to be purchased with points. It usually costs ten yuan to buy a hundred pounds of grain, so almost everyone spent all their earning points just to buy grain. These numbers were used in my home village's "production team" in 1960. Every region in China had different point systems. And if you did not have a residence permit where you were living and working, you could not collect your points or your rations.

GLOSSARY

Ah + name: It is a local custom in south China, especially Guangdong province, that people casually call each other's first name by adding "Ah" in front of a word in the first name. For example, if a girl's name is Mary-Lou, people will call her Ah Lou.

Bad elements: During the Cultural Revolution, "bad element" referred to people who were not in line with the politically correct background, such as the landlords (farm owners), business owners, scholars, and "capitalist roaders."

Brigade: Seven production teams formed a brigade, and a few brigades formed a commune when the People's Communes were formed in China in the late '50s and '60s.

Chiang Kai-shek: was the president of the former Republic of China and chairman of the Kuomintang party who settled down in Taiwan after he lost in the civil war with the communists.

Coupon: It was a commodity purchase certificate issued to city residents by the governments of the People's Republic of China under the planned economy system in the '60s and '70s. In order to control food distribution when there was a shortage, food coupons were required to purchase food including rice, flour, meat, and cooking oil. There were also coupons for other non-food necessities such as fabric, soap, etc.

Dazibao: In Chinese, it means a large word article poster. It was used to criticize and attack someone in public during the Cultural Revolution.

Deng Xiaoping: A reformer who led China toward a market economy after Mao died.

Detention center: is a local "study class" in the brigade office for the young people who engaged in private trading, or whose class consciousness was not in line with the communist doctrine. Only people who had serious offenses were sent to this class. This class lasted for a week or two. In this class, people had to sleep on the straw at night and study Mao's thoughts, current policies, and do self-criticism.

Dongguan: It was a town in Guangdong province; now it is a modern city near Guangzhou City.

Dream of Red Mansions: is one of China's Four Great Classical Novels. It was written sometime in the middle of the 18th century during the Qing dynasty. It is a story of a large, powerful family that reflects the author's, Cao Xueqin's, own life.

Erhu: A Chinese two-stringed bowed musical instrument, also known as the Chinese violin. It is used as a solo instrument as well as in small ensembles and large orchestras.

Fen: Chinese money denomination for a hundredth of a yuan, so it is like a "penny"; the value of a fen was around half the amount of a penny in Mao's era.

Five Black Categories: During the Cultural revolution: landlords, rich peasants, counter-revolutionaries, bad-elements, and rightists were categorized as Five Black.

Four Olds: Old ideas, old culture, old customs, and old habits. There was no clear definition of Four Olds. So the Red Guards destroyed many ancient monuments including national treasures.

Gang of Four: The Gang of Four was the name given to a political faction composed of four top Chinese communist officials, including Mao's wife Jiang Qing, Zhang Chunqiao, Wang Hongwen, and Yao Wenyuan, who came to prominence during the Cultural Revolution (1966–76) and were responsible for directly conducting the Cultural Revolution with a series of treasonous crimes.

Gon An: Chinese police, but Gon An had a lot of civil administration power.

Guangzhou: A big city in southern China, and it is the capital of Guangdong providence.

Journey to the West: A sixteenth-century Chinese novel authored by Wu Cheng'en'. It is a fictional story of the pilgrimage of a Buddhist monk to the "Western Regions" of Central Asia. The monk was protected by three followers, including a monkey king and a pig general. The story is based on an actual pilgrimage journey to India by a Tang Dynasty monk, Xuanzang.

Labor camps/Labor correction: were used in China during the Cultural Revolution as a punishment for people who violated the regulations or had ideology not in the line of communism. The labor correction was conducted in a detention center or labor camp; people who had been labeled as "bad elements" or "Five Black Categories" were sent there to re-educate.

Landlords: refers to farm owners who owned large amounts of farmland, hired workers, and rented the farmland to peasants.

Liang: One Liang is 1/10 of a Chinese pound, equivalent to 1.32 ounces.

Macao: It is an autonomous region on the south coast of China, across the Pearl River Delta from Hong Kong. A Portuguese territory until 1999.

Mu: One acre equivalent of 6.075 mu of land, which is about 0.164 acre.

Nine categories: During the Cultural Revolution, landlords, rich peasants, counter-revolutionaries, bad elements, rightists, traitors, foreign agents, capitalists, and intellectuals (which included teachers) were referred to as the nine categories.

People's Commune: (See Appendix.) To practice communist ideology and remove private ownership, People's Communes were formed during the Great Leap Forward Campaign led by the Chinese government in 1958. In the countryside, a commune was typically formed by many villages called production teams with consolidated agricultural resources, including farmland, farm equipment, tools, and farm animals. All the peasants became members of the Commune and worked for the Commune.

Shaoguan: A town in Guandong province on the border of Hunan and Jiangxi provinces.

Production team: Since the People's Commune campaign in 1958, farmers in China became a member of Commune and worked for the Commune. Members in one village formed a production team as a basic working unit of the Commune.

Public Canteen: During the People's Commune movement, people ate together at a community eatery with a community kitchen for free, which is part of practicing communism.

Red Guards: Students from high schools and universities formed paramilitary units as part of the social movement in the Cultural Revolution. They wore a red armband on their sleeves.

Speculation of profiteering trade: one of the criminal charges for people producing or buying merchandise at low cost and selling it for profit, such as selling farm animals or other farm goods to the black market. From the late '50s to the end of the Mao era, the Chinese government controlled all trade. Private trade of any merchandise was forbidden.

The Three Kingdoms: is a 14th-century historical novel attributed to Luo Guanzhong. It is set in the turbulent years toward the end of the Han dynasty and the Three Kingdoms period in Chinese history. It is considered to be one of the four masterpieces of Chinese classic novels.

Utopian paradise: An imagined place or state of things in which everything is perfect.

The Water Margin: is a 14th-century Chinese novel attributed to Shi Nai'an, also translated as *Outlaws of the Marsh, Tale of the Marshes*, or *All Men Are Brothers*. It is considered one of the four masterpieces of the classic Chinese novels.

Yuan: The monetary unit of China, equal to 100 fen.

Zhongshan: A small city in south China named after the founding father of the Republic of China, Dr. Sun Zhongshen. After the reform of China in the '80s and '90s, Zhongshen rapidly grew into a big city.

Zhou Enlai: Zhou Enlai (Chow Enlai) was the prime minister of the People's Republic of China from 1949 to 1976. He was one of the early leaders of the Chinese communist party.

ABOUT THE AUTHOR

AMY CHAN ZHOU was born in Guangzhou, China, in 1964. She immigrated to the United States in 1979. After graduating from high school in Brooklyn, New York, she went to The State University of New York at Buffalo and The State University of New York College at Old West-bury. She received her B.S. degree in Accounting in 1989. She has worked in various accounting firms and companies from 1989 to 1996. She is currently working in the Maryland public school system.

www.ingramcontent.com/pod-product-compliance
Lightning Source LLC
Chambersburg PA
CBHW030242100426
42812CB00002B/280